PENDULUMS
&INTUITION

PENDULUMS & INTUITION

Practical Advice for Trusting Your Inner Wisdom

KARINA MULLER ✧ LANA GENDLIN

Llewellyn Publications
Woodbury, Minnesota

FIRST EDITION
First Printing, 2024

Book design by R. Brasington
Cover design by Kevin R. Brown
Interior illustrations by Llewellyn Art Department

Pendulums shown in photographs are provided by Lo Scarabeo and
    HeartCentric Divine Creations.

Llewellyn Publications is a registered trademark of Llewellyn Worldwide Ltd.

Library of Congress Cataloging-in-Publication Data (Pending)
ISBN: 978-0-7387-7609-5

Llewellyn Worldwide Ltd. does not participate in, endorse, or have any authority or responsibility concerning private business transactions between our authors and the public.

All mail addressed to the author is forwarded but the publisher cannot, unless specifically instructed by the author, give out an address or phone number.

Any internet references contained in this work are current at publication time, but the publisher cannot guarantee that a specific location will continue to be maintained. Please refer to the publisher's website for links to authors' websites and other sources.

Llewellyn Publications
A Division of Llewellyn Worldwide Ltd.
2143 Wooddale Drive
Woodbury, MN 55125-2989
www.llewellyn.com

Printed in the United States of America

Disclaimer

This book is not intended to provide medical or mental health advice or to take the place of advice and treatment from your primary care provider. Readers are advised to consult their doctors or other qualified healthcare professionals regarding the treatment of their medical or mental health problems. Neither the publisher nor the authors take any responsibility for any possible consequences from any treatment to any person reading or following the information in this book.

The information provided should not be used for diagnosing or treating a health problem or disease in animals, and those seeking personal medical advice for their pets should consult with a licensed veterinarian. Always seek the advice of your veterinarian regarding your pet's medical condition. Do not apply essential oils to pets or pet-related items, as ingestion is harmful to animals.

Contents

FOREWORD

I love pendulums. My first entrée into this amazing tool came through scenes from old movies from the 1940s and 1950s, in which characters swung pocket watches on chains in front of unsuspecting people, putting them into trance states while suggesting, "You are getting very sleepy…" That hypnosis trope became truly overdone and is unfortunately one reason why, to this very day, people distrust hypnotherapy and believe that unscrupulous hypnotists are going around entrancing people without their permission. In reality, the state of hypnosis helps you get in deeper rapport with your own inner being. Brain waves slow down and healing happens. You're actually in more control at those times than you are in full waking consciousness. That magical image remained in my mind until I decided to pursue hypnosis as a career.

In my early hypnosis training, I was taught to work with the pendulum because doing so helps you get control of your unconscious or subconscious mind and bring those inner understandings into better alignment with your conscious waking actions. Training in this way is an excellent idea for anybody, whether they think they will use the pendulum professionally or not. Every person alive, including myself, can always benefit from getting to know themselves better. That's a lifelong pursuit, and the pendulum can be a wonderful partner in helping you uncover the deeper aspects of the self. That's one of the many reasons why I love *Pendulums*

& Intuition: Practical Advice for Trusting Your Inner Wisdom. Lana Gendlin and Karina Muller offer a wealth of resources, sound advice, and exercises within these pages to help you get the most out of this ancient tool.

What I found by working with pendulums is that I felt I had a knack for them. Getting the "rock on a rope" to swing and signify yes or no answers came easy to me. You likely have certain tools or resources that come easy to you also. We all have our own unique gifts and talents, of course, yet that's another thing I appreciate about this book. Lana and Karina show you that with practice and by trying different exercises and experiences to see what resonates best with you, everybody can learn how to utilize a pendulum.

After using my pendulum to gain answers to binary yes or no questions, I later discovered the pendulum could be used for much more when I began using it with my energy healing clients and later with my healing students. We all have an energetic aspect to ourselves that goes beyond our physical bodies. When our energy is out of whack due to the stressors of life, energy healing can bring much needed balance. When I first started doing private practice healing sessions for clients, over twenty years ago now, I was still so new to the practice, I hadn't quite learned to trust myself, so I enlisted the help of my pendulum to ask questions about how best to proceed with the healing sessions—what techniques would be best, what gems and stones or essential oils might be of benefit, and so forth. I found that the pendulum almost always gave me the same answers that were in alignment with my own inner voice, and by seeing those definitive answers in the outer world, the pendulum helped me strengthen my ability to trust myself and my intuition. The more I received pendulum swings that supported my inner knowing, the more I learned to trust myself.

Eventually, I began teaching energy healing to others. I happen to love teaching healing to beginners. It's so very exciting to watch someone sense the energetic aspects of another human being or animal for the first time. That's an aha moment that is a privilege to see firsthand. Like me, beginning energy healing students also need practice and positive feedback in order to learn how to trust their own intuition. They also must develop the skill of recognizing the life force in themselves, other people, and all living beings and to know how, when, and where to proceed. There's no better way to see how energy moves and to receive intuitive feedback to help clients during healing sessions than the pendulum.

One of the most amazing examples of using pendulums in healing involves the seven chakra centers, the swirling vortexes of light-colored energy that exist within each of us. These colored vortexes match the rainbow spectrum and should be open and spinning equally in order to have balance in life. Using a pendulum can help you visually see if someone's energy and chakra centers are open or closed. The results of using pendulums in this way can be quite dramatic. I'll never forget the first time I saw a pendulum that remained completely still while I passed it over a client's body. I was shocked! That meant that for whatever reason, their energy was completely blocked and the dear soul truly needed the energy healing.

Aside from detecting opened and closed energies, pendulums can also help you get things moving in the right direction. In such cases where chakras need more opening, the pendulum can help direct you to open them so balance and peace are restored to body, mind, and spirit.

Once I developed my skills in answering simple questions and opening energy, I eventually came to understand the most important task a pendulum can help with: understanding the self. There is no better tool to help you visually see the highest good and purpose within yourself than the pendulum. Far beyond simple questions about where to go to dinner tonight or what to wear to the party, the pendulum can help you answer some of the biggest questions you have about your soul, your purpose, and your reason for being.

In these times of instant gratification, it's easier now than ever to seek answers outside of the self, whether that be through psychic readings, films, or other content. With a pendulum as your ultimate friend and ally, you can use the advice in this book and learn to quiet the mind and engage with the depths of your own being. What you'll find is that your pendulum will tell you something that even your most well-meaning friends may not—the truth.

Truth is subjective and differs for each person, yet within you and I are the answers that will yield the best and brightest results for us on an individual level. What's good for you is not necessarily anything that would work for me. We're all so different. When you're able to tune in to your own soul, you can find direction and guidance that is specific to you and you alone. When you feel stuck and need someone who understands your inner being, having the pendulum is a true gift that yields huge results on the path of life. When you learn to trust yourself and go with what you know to be correct within the depths of your soul, you become truly empowered.

I can't tell you the number of times I've asked my pendulum questions and received the answer that I did not want to hear. If I wanted a yes and received a no, I learned that following the pendulum even when I could not see the final outcome of doing so at the present vantage point always yielded a good result. Your pendulum connects you with your higher self or soul essence. What is good for your soul in the long run is not always readily apparent. After messing up many things in my younger days, I finally realized that following this higher guidance with the help of my pendulum brought great rewards and a deep sense of trust for myself, which is a gift of the spirit that remains steadfast throughout my life.

Who in our lives has our best interest in mind? If we're lucky, we have supportive family and friends, and yet even they can often steer us toward outcomes based on their experiences rather than our own. Turning to the self and the soul while visually seeing the answers you seek is an amazing gift to give to yourself. Working with the material in *Pendulums & Intuition* is a perfect starting place to begin your journey to deepen the relationship and trust you have with yourself. If you're already a longtime student of the pendulum, this book will be an amazing refresher filled with new twists on how to receive more accurate answers using some of the fantastic charts and diagrams Lana and Karina have developed for you to use.

All these reasons and more are why I absolutely love *Pendulums & Intuition* by my dear friends Lana and Karina. Like me, they also agree with the ideas of empowering the individual to find their own truth and answers from within in order to create a greater connection with the highest good for all concerned. I highly recommend this book to all seekers who long to find the right answers to big questions while making a loving connection with themselves.

—Shelley A. Kaehr, PhD, author of *The Goddess Discovered* and
Heal Your Ancestors to Heal Your Life

INTRODUCTION

What if we told you that you could have a personal amazing guidance assistant (AGA) with you at all times? This friend and ally would be dedicated to you and only you. For example, when you're trying to determine whether it's time to leave your nine-to-five job to pursue the dream of opening your own upcycled goods boutique. Or when you're deciding what to wear on a blind date with someone you're rather excited to meet. Perhaps you're painting your bedroom and can't seem to nail down the right color. How about when you're grocery shopping and unsure if a certain food is good for your body? This list can go on and on...

Of course, it would be incredible to know with certainty what the right decision is for you in the moment and be able to follow through with it. How extraordinary would it be to get "unstuck" in moments of doubt, fear, and self-judgment or find the clarity that you need under difficult circumstances? If you're like most people, you've probably been shaped and conditioned to believe certain views about yourself based on your family of origin, environment, and numerous other factors. You may still be living out the same limiting stories from childhood.

There *is* a tool that can help you overcome these beliefs by learning what is true for you and not anyone else. This tool works visually, quickly, easily, and effectively, and it's also portable and fun to work with. Would you be curious to learn more about it? If you're read-ing this book, you probably answered yes.

This tool is a pendulum. The pendulum is an ideal tool to check in with yourself and discover your inner wisdom and guidance. And the key to unlock-ing a pendulum's power is the intuition inside of you. We all have intuition—it is our superpower. Your intuition, via your subconscious mind, is your very own amazing guidance assistant, and it is available to you at all times because it is an inherent part of you that resides inside your mind, body, heart, and soul. For many, it may often seem tough to access your intuition, or you may find it difficult to trust it. In this book, we're going to show you quite the opposite.

Pendulums are more than an object that is used to look within for answers. Often mistaken for a piece of jewelry, this small, beautiful tool is symbolic of a larger shift that is happening on a collective and global scale. Many refer to this time in our history as an epoch that is moving humanity toward a higher state of being, a collective consciousness that is ascending into a New Earth—a world in which life is lighter, freer, more joyful, and enlightened.

You may have heard of pendulums before but may not know how to use one or why you should. Perhaps you already have a pendulum and would like to expand your knowledge and practice. Either way, you've come to the right place. We believe everyone should have *at least* one pendulum. Pendulums can be simple, intricate, or anything in between. Some like to use a ring or paper clip attached to a string. You can even use a necklace as a pendulum. It is a very personal tool, and as such, having a pendulum that you love will strengthen your connection with it—and with yourself. Whether you use it for guidance, healing, energy work, or dowsing, it's crucial to know that the pendulum is not what holds the power and magic on its own. The power is within you! Without you, a pendulum is just an object.

Over the last few years, we have met and spoken with thousands of people who are looking to go deeper and connect with their inner knowing. What has surprised us the most are the special, personal connections we make by sharing our message about pendulums and intuition with the world, as well as how much people love using them, proving how needed they are right now. People are definitely curious about pendulums. The reason why is that they are find-ing answers buried deep within their subconscious mind to reveal the guidance within. It's as if they are having an internal dialogue with their own soul.

Our Journey

This book is about deep learning, friendship, and discovering new beginnings through the power of intuition with the use of a pendulum. We are the quintessential examples of two women letting go of external expectations from our families, friends, and coworkers and tapping into our inner guidance to navigate our lives. By strengthening the connection to our intuition and taking action on the guidance from that inner voice, we have been able to transform our lives to live every day in joy, happiness, and freedom. Our careers and personal lives are enormous sources of fulfillment for us. Both of us are corporate and nonprofit recoverees who learned that if something is in need of change, we are willing to surrender and allow our intuition to lead the way. It wasn't always that way. We spent decades in somewhat fulfilling careers and relationships that ultimately drained us.

Our ups and downs left us searching for work that truly sparked us and had meaning, both professionally and personally. When we envisioned our ideal careers and took action to bring them to fruition, we created HeartCentric, LLC. We were divinely guided down this path, but we also leaned into our intuition and followed the yellow brick road that our AGAs laid out. While doing this came with much uncertainty, we pushed through the fear and challenges. We continue on our paths to move through feelings of fear and choose love every day. It's not always easy, but it is thrilling, invigorating, and fulfilling.

When the two of us met during the COVID pandemic while obtaining our life coaching certifications, we had no idea that we'd find our purpose by running a business called HeartCentric. Our work is centered on handcrafting pendulums and coaching clients on how to use them to connect to their intuition. It took only a few short months for us to cocreate with the universe (a term we will use throughout the book to refer to a higher form of consciousness) and set the path to manifest HeartCentric into reality.

Our greatest joy is seeing the look on someone's face the first time they try using a pendulum. It's a cocktail of astonishment, awe, excitement, and newfound awareness. We love educating those who are curious about pendulums and demonstrating how to use them. Connecting with people in this way is a big part of our approach to introducing pendulums into their lives. The energy that these experiences bring is tough to convey in a two-dimensional, written platform. It's truly magical.

About This Book

This book will explore pendulums and how they help you connect within, how to select your perfect pendulum and what to do to get started, how to care for your pendulum (and yourself), divination, practical uses for pendulums, what to do when you need troubleshooting, resources and practice exercises, and our stories. Think of this book as your companion on your journey to yourself!

Many books about pendulums are written from the perspective of a mystic, psychic, or spiritual healer. Our book is written from the perspective of two women on a spiritual path. While we consider ourselves lightworkers who have been guided to help others heal, we have spent decades working in business—from corporate and nonprofits to startups. Ours is a practical guide written by everyday women for everyday people. It allows anyone who's curious to tap into their inner wisdom in an accessible and approachable way. This book sets the context to learn about pendulums from a combination of historical, energetic, and scientific perspectives. We are also the makers of all our pendulums, which are genuinely "handcrafted with love and good vibes" (our tagline). These are works of art and spiritual tools for healing and divination.

A pendulum can be used in many different ways for many purposes. We all have the potential to be the best AGA for ourselves. We will say this throughout the book, "No one knows what is best for you better than you." The key to activating your superpower is knowing how to unleash it and use it. No matter what walk of life you're from, regardless of age, gender, nationality, socioeconomic status, or education level, anyone who has the desire to become their own AGA can do so. Together, we will show you how to connect to your intuition with a pendulum, no matter what questions you have. There is no limit to your potential to live your most authentic life every single day. By the time you finish this book, you will be on your way to becoming your most trusted AGA and relying on yourself for answers.

The reason we wrote this book is because we want to share information about the power of the pendulum with as many people as possible. By doing this work, we are helping you, and those in your circle of influence, connect with your intuition, claim your power, and live your best life. We hope you will share what you've learned about pendulums and their value with others whom you inspire. One by one, we are helping each other reach our own optimal potential. Imagine a world where people are joyful and feel free to authentically be who they are meant to be. What a world that would be. We are honored that you are here with us on our journey. We truly believe the possibilities are endless!

One of our goals with this book is to bring valuable information about pendulums to the masses. We are demystifying and destigmatizing this tool by normalizing it and bringing it into the mainstream. Through our in-person events and educational workshops, we have collected numerous stories directly from our customers about how they are using this tool firsthand. We share their stories about healing and empowerment in this book. We are grateful to have the opportunity to be a part of this journey at this profound time in history.

Our mission is simple: empowering people to connect to their intuition with the help of a pendulum. We believe this ancient tool belongs in the modern world, especially as we leave old, outdated dogmas behind and enter a New Earth. There is no better time to bring awareness of this tool to the mainstream—for healing, for navigating life's ups and downs, and most of all for empowering people to live their best life. We are all creative and intuitive beings, and we already have all the answers we seek inside of us. Tapping into that wisdom is like discovering a gold mine. When we learn to deeply connect with ourselves and go within for answers, we start making decisions from the heart instead of the mind. Heart-centered decision-making ultimately takes us to a place of joyous living. And if more people can live in their joy, all of humanity benefits. We invite you to join us to create a lasting impact on the world!

Discovering Our Innate Creativity

We feel extremely passionate about bringing pendulums into the modern world in a broader context because we know they have the ability to empower people to connect with their intuition, which is tied to their creativity. As human beings, creativity is a part of our DNA. We are all innately creative. It is when we align our hearts with our minds and access our creativity that we are able to bring ideas to life and bring them to market faster. Getting into "creative flow" to help improve our lives and live in our creative spirit is of the utmost importance to us.

Are you ready to connect within to live your most authentic and aligned life? Then you've found the right tool to help you. We can think about our dreams, but at some point, we have to take action. Clearly, our intuition has guided us on the right path—and it can do the same for you. We are excited to take you on a journey of self-exploration using an ancient tool for modern times.

Chapter 1
SETTING THE STAGE

Before we dive into your exciting pendulum journey, we would like to take a moment to first set the stage about the importance of intuition, the power of the subconscious mind, benefits of self-care, and basic knowledge about the clairs. You do not have to be a spiritual teacher to use a pendulum effectively and responsibly. We witnessed our own intuitive abilities develop at lightning speed when we made a conscious shift to allow our intuition to have a voice and let go of our own limiting beliefs. For Karina, it showed up as releasing the need to make mostly data-driven decisions. For Lana, it was the shedding of a long-held belief of "it's not in the stars for me." The path that opened up for us has been paved with rewarding experiences that fill our hearts with joy on a daily basis. When you open yourself up to your intuition, you open yourself up to endless possibilities.

What is intuition? When Oprah Winfrey describes intuition, she talks about "trusting the still, small voice" that is almost "more of a feeling" or "a whispery sensation that pulsates just beneath the surface." For her, it has been all about trusting her instincts and allowing them to guide her in the direction that is best for her.[1]

---

1 Oprah Winfrey, "What Oprah Knows for Sure about Trusting Her Intuition," *O, The Oprah Magazine*, August 2011, https://www.oprah.com/spirit/oprah-on-trusting-her-intuition-oprahs-advice-on-trusting-your-gut.

Many people who had a part to play in changing the world relied heavily on their intuition for groundbreaking inventions. Think Albert Einstein, Nicola Tesla, Steve Jobs, and many others. Albert Einstein's theory of relativity is now renowned as a pinnacle of modern-day physics. This famous quote often attributed to Einstein sums it up perfectly: "The intuitive mind is a sacred gift and a rational mind is a faithful servant."[2] Einstein faced a lot of criticism from the scientific community for following his intuition and challenging centuries of scientific work. Another Einstein quote that we admire is "All great achievements of science must start from intuitive knowledge."[3]

In his 2005 Stanford commencement speech, Steve Jobs, American business magnate, inventor, and investor most notably known for cofounding Apple, Inc., credits his intuition for finding the path leading to his career success. In his speech, he encourages the graduates to "have the courage to follow [their] heart and intuition. They somehow already know what you truly want to become." In his personal experience, Jobs chose to trust his intuitive abilities, and this approach never let him down.[4]

Your subconscious mind is what activates your intuition. When you connect with a reservoir of memories of past experiences that are buried in your subconscious, you gain access to information that can help you navigate your life in the present moment.

The Importance of Intuition

The pendulum is a perfect introductory tool to help people connect to their intuition. When we tap into our intuitive wisdom and follow the guidance that we receive, our life begins to flow. Obstacles that seem overwhelming become easier to overcome. Problems that seem impossible to solve turn into small challenges and bumps on the road. Intuition is a guiding light that enables us to step onto our optimal path in life and discover endless opportunities that are available to us each and every day.

---

2   Ruth Umoh, "Steve Jobs and Albert Einstein Both Attributed Their Extraordinary Success to This Personality Trait," CNBC, last modified June 30, 2017, https://www.cnbc.com/2017/06/29/steve-jobs-and-albert-einstein-both-attributed-their-extraordinary-success-to-this-personality-trait.html.

3   Alice Calaprice, ed., The Ultimate Quotable Einstein (Princeton, NJ: Princeton University Press, 2011), 435.

4   Steve Jobs, commencement address, Stanford University, June 12, 2005, https://news.stanford.edu/2005/06/12/youve-got-find-love-jobs-says/.

Why haven't we been taught to utilize this superpower more often? Historically, our society has trained us to honor and respect our logical minds and doubt our intuitive guidance. But when we allow our intuition to have a voice, our logical mind, or our ego, steps aside and allows our heart to have its say. When we act from our heart's desires, we honor what is truly best for us. We can always ask our friends, family, or the internet for guidance. But when we ask our hearts for guidance, we will always receive the answers that serve our own highest good. After all, nobody knows what's best for you better than you.

Our intuitive mind resides in our subconscious. Essentially, the subconscious is a repository for all your experiences and controls almost everything in your life. It stores your beliefs, memories, feelings, emotions, gifts, and talents. Everything that you have seen, done, experienced, felt, thought, and imagined is also stored in your subconscious. Connecting with the power of the subconscious mind can open up our lives to gifts beyond our wildest dreams.

The opportunity we are faced with on a daily basis is figuring out how to gain access to all of that wisdom already inside of us. Working with a pendulum will allow you to consistently tap into that guidance and learn to trust it. Before we dive into how to use a pendulum, let's explore what we mean when we talk about connecting to your inner wisdom, or intuition. After all, this is not something that we see with our physical eyes. Rather, it's a feeling…an inner knowing. Fundamentally, we're asking you to connect your mind with your physical body and your heart.

The human body has three distinct networks that connect to each other: the head, the gut, and the heart. Often called the "three brains," these core processing systems and organs control our physical health, thoughts, and feelings. Our intuitive knowings comes from our heart-gut-soul connection, not from our conscious minds.[5]

For the last forty years, the HeartMath Institute has been doing extensive research on the topic of heart "coherence," which is defined as a high performance and healthy state—physically, emotionally, mentally, and spiritually—that brings out the very best in us. The institute's studies found that "the heart actually sends more signals to the brain than the brain sends to the heart! Moreover,

---

5   Joe Mechlinski, "Understanding the Three 'Brains' in Our Body (and Their Critical Role at Work),"
     Medium, September 5, 2018, https://medium.com/@joemechlinski_9502/understanding-the
     -three-brains-in-our-body-and-their-critical-role-at-work-d1715ae62bff.

these heart signals have a significant effect on brain function—influencing emotional processing as well as higher cognitive faculties such as attention, perception, memory, and problem-solving. In other words, not only does the heart respond to the brain, but the brain continuously responds to the heart."[6]

While our minds think and work through problems based on the evidence that we acquire, our intuitive knowledge connects to awareness at an energetic level. The intuitive knowing can't decipher any limitations. It is a radar for all the goodness not limited by the rational mind's constraints. When we allow our intuition to have a greater influence on our lives, we begin to form a stronger connection between our left brain and our right brain. This connection fires up the neurons that encourage creativity, imagination, play, and a state of joyful being.

The energetic heart, as studied by the HeartMath Institute, contains innate intelligence, not learned intelligence that is stored in the conscious mind. The energetic heart is what drives heart-mind coherence. When the heart is open and is influencing the mind, our level of awareness expands exponentially. Heart-mind coherence allows individuals to reach a higher level of conscious awareness.[7]

How does all this information relate to your work with a pendulum? It goes back to the wealth of wisdom, guided by our hearts, that is always available to us. When we listen to the wisdom of our hearts, we allow heart coherence to take place. The pendulum is a wonderful tool that allows us to ask powerful questions and tap into the innate wisdom already available to us. Once we extract what we need, we can begin to listen and act on the wisdom, which will create a more positive mental and emotional state. Living in this positivity allows us to feel good, live with harmony and joy, and perform optimally in all aspects of our lives.

---

6   "The Science of HeartMath," HeartMath, accessed September 19, 2023, https://www.heartmath.com/science/.

7   "The Energetic Heart Is Unfolding," HeartMath, July 22, 2010, https://www.heartmath.org/articles-of-the-heart/science-of-the-heart/the-energetic-heart-is-unfolding/.

The Science Behind the Pendulum

For all human beings, 95 percent of our brain activity is in the subconscious. Our subconscious mind is the host to our automatic body functions such as breathing, emotions, habits, creativity, and long-term memories. Only 5 percent of our brain's cognitive activity is allocated to the conscious mind.[8] We are going to focus on how to extract all that useful information buried in your subconscious and bring it to the surface.

There are many ways to tap into your subconscious. Meditation, yoga, tarot and oracle cards, muscle testing, visualization—these are but a few of the many ways to access your subconscious. Our preferred method is the pendulum. The pendulum gives the subconscious mind a voice through a visual, energetic movement, and it does it faster than any other method we know of.

Working with a pendulum is the process of getting our conscious and subconscious minds to speak to each other. We often refer to Freud's iceberg model to describe the difference between the conscious and the subconscious mind. Freud's psychoanalytic theory of personality states that everything we recognize is what the conscious mind is composed of. This part of the iceberg is the tip that is visible above the water. The subconscious is represented by the majority of the iceberg, which is submerged below the surface. Freud believed that the bulk of our mind's content is found in the subconscious. This rich and powerful content is available to anyone willing to look beneath the surface and put in the work.[9]

The conscious mind is defined as the part of the mind that is responsible for rationalizing, paying attention, logical thinking, and reasoning. It is also known to control all our day-to-day activities done on a voluntary basis. The conscious mind is the gatekeeper. It keeps track and communicates with the outside world and inner self through receptive sensations, thoughts, speech, pictures, writing, and physical activities.

According to the latest research studies, the conscious mind has been found to be highly dependent on the subconscious mind, which decides on

---

8   Thomas Nail, "Most Brain Activity Is Background Noise'—and That's Upending Our Understanding of Consciousness," *Salon*, February 20, 2021, https://www.salon.com/2021/02/20/most-brain-activity-is-background-noise-cognitive-flux-consciousness-brain-activity-research/.

9   Saul Mcleod, "Freud's Theory of the Unconscious Mind," Simply Psychology, last modified October 24, 2023, https://www.simplypsychology.org/unconscious-mind.html.

how humans function as a whole.[10] The subconscious is defined as the section of the mind that is responsible for all the involuntary actions and accessible information which is being received in day-to-day life. For example, the continuous processes of breathing, blood circulation, and heartbeat are known to be controlled by an individual's subconscious mind. All our emotions are controlled by the subconscious mind. This is why we feel negative emotions like sadness, fear, and anxiety even without wanting to experience them in response to various circumstances.

The subconscious mind is also known to be the storage center where individual beliefs, attitudes, and long-term memories are stacked. All day, every day, you are bombarded with an endless amount of information. Your conscious mind cannot review and process everything. The subconscious mind is the filter that processes everything and lets through only what is relevant at that very moment in time to your conscious mind.[11]

The Power of the Subconscious Mind

The subconscious mind is extremely powerful. It willingly acts on thoughts that are experienced with tremendous conviction and desire. When you allow yourself to imagine and feel your deepest desires, your subconscious will open all available channels of communication to your conscious mind. When these doors open, they allow inside the information you need to make your dreams come true. Empowering your subconscious mind to help you reach your desires opens up all the opportunities in life that enable you to achieve what you want.

Your mind and your programming may be the only obstacles keeping you from realizing your full potential. To overcome these barriers, it is necessary to have a conscious relationship with the subconscious mind and master it. In order for the subconscious to execute the best possible program, we have to reprogram negative beliefs or patterns that have persisted.

The subconscious mind speaks in feelings, dreams, images, and sensations. It captures all the information that comes to us through our five senses. When

10 Andrew Bundson, Kenneth Richman, and Elizabeth Kensinger, "Consciousness as a Memory System," Cognitive and Behavioral Neurology 25, no. 4 (December 2022): 263–97, doi:10.1097/WNN.000000000000031.

11 Embogama, "Difference between Conscious and Unconscious Mind," Pediaa, August 5, 2016, https://pediaa.com/difference-between-conscious-and-subconscious-mind/.

we program our subconscious mind to focus on spotting and bringing us opportunities aligned with our highest, most optimal goals, our subconscious mind will get to work. Powering that goal with strong emotional desire and total faith in the outcome creates a stream of opportunities that start showing up in our conscious awareness. Our subconscious is there to serve us, so think carefully about what information you consume and how you speak to yourself.

The pendulum is an extremely effective tool to tap into our subconscious because we can see and feel it working with our own energy. Pendulums translate what our intuition tells us into yes and no movements when we ask questions that we seek answers to. As we begin asking the pendulum questions, we extract what is buried deep within our subconscious mind and bring it into conscious awareness.

Pendulums have been around for centuries, yet the majority of mainstream society knows little to nothing about their use and value. There are skeptics out there who are adamant that the pendulum moves because the person holding it is moving it. And they're right... sort of. At face value, there is truth to this. The distinction is that the person holding the pendulum is *not* aware that they are moving it.

When we dig deeper into what is going on, there is a scientific *and* energetic explanation around how and why the pendulum moves and what it means in relation to your life and awareness. That communication happens through the ideomotor reflex. The ideomotor effect, also called ideomotor reflex or ideomotor response, is when inner guidance causes your body to slightly move without you being aware of it. The muscles moving in your arm are triggered by your subconscious brain activity.[12] So by asking your pendulum a yes or no question, your pendulum is responding to what your intuition already knows subconsciously. The subconscious mind is sending a signal to the brain, which then sends a signal down the arm and prompts the movement of the hand. These reflexes are barely noticeable because our bodies are making this movement involuntarily.

A French chemist named Michel Eugène Chevreul, best known for his contributions to science, medicine, and art in the nineteenth century, researched

---

12 Jay A. Olson, Ewalina Jeyanesan, and Amir Raz, "Ask the Pendulum: Personality Predictors of Ideomotor Performance," *Neuroscience of Consciousness* 1 (2017): nix014, https://www.ncbi.nlm.nih.gov/pmc/articles/PMC5858027/.

this phenomenon extensively. Chevreul's pioneering research led to our under-standing of how the pendulum works from a scientific perspective. His findings concluded that it is indeed our thoughts and intentions that send a signal to the brain, which is transmitted by the subconscious to the appropriate muscles, causing micromovements that are not seen by the naked eye and communi-cated via a pendulum.[13]

Enriching Our Subconscious

As we begin appreciating the guidance our intuitive mind provides to help us live in our most optimal existence, we must remember to continuously upgrade that database of knowledge with new learnings and experiences. There are some simple ways that we can continuously pursue the quest for knowledge and therefore achieve growth of our intuitive abilities. One of those ways is to engage in hobbies. Have you ever considered trying something new that you've never done before? Perhaps it's a pottery class or a trip somewhere you've never been. These different experiences allow us the opportunity to view the world in new ways, notice new possibilities, and develop innovative solutions to everyday problems.

New experiences may feel uncomfortable at first. To live fully, we must be willing to step into discomfort and challenge ourselves to grow and expand our intuitive Rolodex of information. Change can be difficult and cause fear and anxiety for some. Those are natural, human reactions in life. However, when we focus on staying in our comfort zone too much, we limit ourselves from expanding our possibilities. Life is about exploring the full range of human experiences. By allowing ourselves to fully experience pain and pleasure, chal-lenges and solutions, suffering and satisfaction, we strengthen the knowledge, empathy, and skills for true expansion of our intuitive storehouse.

Your pendulum can help you gain confidence in the guidance you are receiving. As a result, you are constantly enriching the subconscious mind in a positive way.

---

13   Philip D. Shenefelt, "Ideomotor Signaling: From Divining Spiritual Messages to Discerning Subcon-scious Answers During Hypnosis and Hypnoanalysis, A Historical Perspective," *American Journal of Clinical Hypnosis* 53, no. 3 (January 2011): 157–67, doi:10.1080/00029157.2011.10401754.

Self-Care

Another factor that is imperative for a deep connection to intuition is ongoing self-care. We will get the most clarity, wisdom, and the deepest connection when we feel our best—physically, emotionally, and mentally. When we prioritize self-care in our lives, we are better equipped to go on a journey of self-discovery, energetic replenishment, insightful guidance, optimal solutions, and ultimately, great joy and happiness.

The process is simple. Think of the acronym PYT:

1. P is for *put*. Put yourself first.
2. Y is for *you*. Go to yourself for solutions to the challenges you face.
3. T is for *trust*: When the solution shows up from your inner guidance or intuition, learn to trust it and follow it if it feels right. You'll know.

Let's elaborate on what we mean by P for *put*: "Put yourself first." It's a simple formula. Try to ensure that you fill your cup first before filling others'. Most of us are familiar with the phrase "You can't pour from an empty cup." If we prioritize self-care, we will do a much better job taking care of others in our lives. The best way to motivate others is to teach by example. So by modeling that self-care is important, we teach others to do the same. Eventually, they will be more likely to follow your lead. It's a win-win!

What exactly is self-care? There is a plethora of books, articles, and videos about self-care, so we are not going to reinvent the wheel in this book. We provide suggestions in the recommended resources section at the end of this book. At the most basic level, self-care is fueling your body and mind by getting plenty of rest, exercise, and good, nourishing food. Take your vitamins, get out in nature, meditate, and drink plenty of water. And do all of the above every single day.

Now let's explore Y for *you*: "Go to yourself for solutions to the challenges you face." When it comes to solving problems, we are the ones who are best equipped to solve the challenges that we face in our lives. You may get tired of us repeating "all the answers you're seeking are already inside you" over and over and over in this book. As life coaches, we deeply believe this statement to be true. When you source your own answers, they will hold so much more meaning to you than the advice you may get from your friends and family. It's highly likely that those around you offering advice mean well and wish you great success, but they are looking at your situation through their own perspectives, experiences, feelings, and learnings. Only you know what is best for you.

Next, let's dig into T for *trust*: "When the solution shows up from your inner guidance or intuition, learn to trust it and follow it if it feels right." Sometimes the answers to our challenges show up right away. Other times, they may show up a few hours later, the next day, the following week, or sometimes months later. But if you truly want the answers to come, keep paying attention to your intuition. This is where your pendulum practice comes in. We will explore how to do this in detail later in this book. The answers may not show up at the particular moment you want them to, but it's probable they will show up eventually. Patience is key.

Now for the best part. When the answer does show up, notice how you feel about it. Does it feel good? If it does, it's highly likely the right answer for you. If it doesn't feel good, then it's not the right answer. It really can be that simple.

So what do you do with answers that feel *really* good? Act on them! Make appropriate decisions and take action. Your pendulum is always available to you to double-check, confirm, dig deeper, or test another option. Trust the guidance and watch the magic that is your life unfold right in front of you. Your journey to self-discovery is underway. So buckle in for the ride of your life.

The Clairs

What if it's not that simple for you? Where is the information coming from? These are questions that you may be asking. Learning how to tune in to your "clairs" and really listen to your intuition is a skill that can be developed and is worth exploring. Clairs are your body's way of directing you toward your own psychic abilities.

Have you ever had a gut feeling that something just isn't right when you walk into a room? Or have you experienced déjà vu? Does your body react with tingles or goosebumps when you experience a moment that powerfully resonates with you? This is your intuition—or higher self and guides (see chapter 5)—communicating with you to send you messages and guidance. We are all born with psychic abilities. Some of us are more in tune with those abilities and use them naturally, while others may have to listen more intently and develop them, which can take time. How your higher self communicates with you requires paying attention to the spiritual frequencies happening all around you. Think of it as tuning in to your favorite spiritual radio station. Let's take a look at the most dominant clairs.

Clairvoyance: Clear or Psychic Vision

Do you have lucid dreams, visualize stories playing out in your head, or have mental images flash into your awareness? If you have a vivid sense of how you see the world through your mind's eye, you will have a tendency toward clairvoyance. You may also be able to see colors in energy fields and auras, see future events, and gain knowledge about people and things. Some people have the ability to see spirits who have crossed over and other guides, angels, and beings. If this best describes how you receive information, this is your dominant psychic ability. Your spirit guides may communicate with you through your clairvoyance.

Clairaudience: Clear or Psychic Hearing

If you are able to learn about future events, the day-to-day, and people through sounds, whispers, and words, you are most likely clairaudient. Clairaudient individuals often hear and experience sounds with profound depth and significant meaning. They may be able to hear and perceive sounds that others find muffled or can't hear at all, and recall circumstances through music, subtle pitched sounds, and voices rather than remembering them through images, feelings, or smells. Oftentimes, their higher self and guides communicate with them by information simply popping into their mind.

Clairsentience: Clear or Psychic Feeling/Sensing

If you empathize very easily with others, deeply feel what others are experiencing or expressing, and are highly sensitive to the emotions of others around you, clairsentience may be your dominant clair. Clairsentient people often feel chills running up their spine, strong gut feelings regarding something or someone, or butterflies in their stomachs. If this sounds like your dominant clair, you may feel or sense changes in the energy of spaces and the vibes of people around you. If you're someone who is highly sensitive and in tune with your feelings and the feelings of others, you may be a great natural healer or caregiver. Clairsentient people may feel drained after being in a large crowd or spending time with others. Does this sound like you? If so, be careful to protect your own energy and make time to replenish it regularly.

Claircognizance: Clear or Psychic Knowing

If you often receive thoughts, ideas, and concepts that feel like they have been suddenly downloaded into your mind, it is likely that you are claircognizant. Tuning in to the wisdom and information that you get from your higher self and guides is a skill to develop in order to determine what is truly claircognizance and what is your own mind chatter. If this is your dominant clair, you may come up with creative solutions to problems or ideas for new inventions that seem to come out of nowhere. This clair requires a great deal of trust and faith in the universe, as there is no clear explanation for why we suddenly "know" what we do.

Clairgustance: Clear or Psychic Tasting

This clair is described as the ability to taste a substance that isn't actually there. Individuals with clairgustance sometimes report tasting a favorite food or drink of a relative or loved one who has crossed over. If you are a detective or an investigator, an example of clairgustance may be you experiencing odd flavors in your mouth that align with specific clues, such as the taste of blood. A heightened sense of taste can also lead individuals to become great chefs or foodies. They will often connect with what they put into their bodies on a deeper level than others.

Clairalience: Clear or Psychic Smelling

Do you ever smell something that reminds you of a certain situation or somebody? If you recall events or experience things through a heightened sense of smell, you may be clairalient. While less common, this clair is when you have the ability to smell something that is not in your surroundings. Both clairalience and clairgustance can be highly personal and bring different meanings to the individual depending on their own life experience.

Putting It All Together

Most of us have more than one clair that our intuition, our higher self, and spirit guides like to communicate with us through. We'll explore the higher self and spirit guides a little more in chapter 5. It may take us a period of time to learn how to discern one clair from the other. For example, it's easy to confuse clairsentience (clear feeling) with claircognizance (clear knowing) because a "knowing" will often come with a reaction in the body (a gut feeling). Often our psychic gifts work together to provide an understanding of what we are meant to receive. Over time and with practice, you will be able to distinguish the difference for you. When you're ready to determine your dominant clairs and you've learned how to work with your pendulum in chapter 4, try doing the following exercise.

Exercise
DETERMINE YOUR DOMINANT CLAIRS

Clairs can help you get in tune with your own psychic abilities. Determining your dominant clairs with the help of a pendulum will show you how your psychic gifts work to provide an understanding of the information we are meant to receive. Please refer to page 48 if you need to learn how to calibrate your pendulum before you get started.

Begin by sitting down comfortably in a space where you will not be disturbed or distracted. A great option is to do this exercise in nature. Scan your environment, mentally noting as many details and feelings as you can for a few minutes. Then, close your eyes and focus on your breath. Breathe deeply and slowly as you mentally review what caught your attention as you were scanning your surroundings. Open your eyes and write down what stood out to you. What did you notice? Was it the sight of something? Maybe it was the smell or sound? Did you suddenly have a thought that almost felt like a fact popped into your head? Based on what you noticed, look back over the descriptions of each clair. Select which clairs resonated the strongest and are most dominant for you. Reflect on how your intuition and guides may be communicating with you via the various clairs, and write them down in your journal.

Now take out your pendulum, calibrate it, and hover your pendulum over each clair on the chart on the next page. With each clair, ask the pendulum if it is your dominant clair. For example, if clairsentience is on your list, ask, "Is clairsentience my dominant clair?"

If you receive a yes to more than one clair, ask if one is more dominant than another. Keep going and ask whatever questions you're curious about in relation to your clairs. For example, ask which clair is in your optimal interest to develop further at this time or if the timing is right to learn more about your psychic abilities. There's no limit to what you can learn about yourself and your gifts. This exercise will help steer you on the most optimal path for you at this point in your journey of self-exploration. And the more you practice noticing how you're receiving information, the more you'll develop your psychic abilities. Check in with your pendulum to confirm what you're learning and trust where your intuition is guiding you.

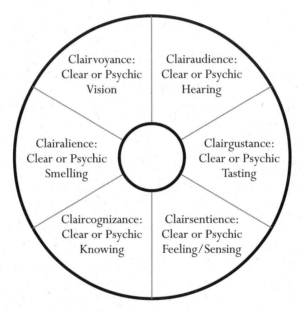

Figure 1: Dominant clairs chart

Chapter 2
WHAT IS A PENDULUM?

Pendulums are tools that help you connect with your intuition and access information buried in your subconscious, the wisest part of your being. They are made from various materials, such as crystals, gemstones, metals, and wood. Anything can be a pendulum as long as it's weighted and hangs from a string. Pendulums work with your energy to access your subconscious mind and extract the answers you seek. But first you have to calibrate your pendulum to understand how it moves to show you what your individual yes, no, maybe, and not now movements look like.

Pendulums are powerful, tactile tools that we can see and feel working with our own energy. They translate what our intuition tells us into movements when we ask questions that we seek answers to. As we begin asking questions and seeking responses through the pendulum, we extract what is buried deep within our subconscious mind and bring it into conscious awareness. When we pay attention to this inner guidance, our lives start to flow more easily. Getting into the flow state allows us to step into our power and live each and every day with joy and happiness.

To do this, we must reach beyond the rational part of our conscious mind. Although it may seem that the pendulum has a mind of its own, it is important to remember that the pendulum is just a tool. It is *you* who is using the tool to access the guidance already within you. Essentially, using a pendulum allows us to have an energetic conversation with ourselves. The pendulum is often likened to that of a radio transmitter. It's a conduit that carries information from your subconscious mind and connects with your heart, where your intuition resides. It then transfers that information to create a physical and visual movement. This unlocks the true nature of your intuition and opens your mind to different perspectives.

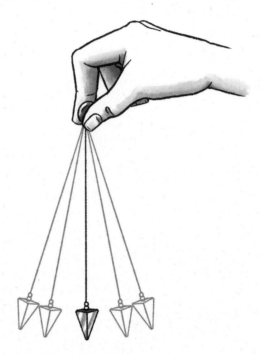

Figure 2: How to hold your pendulum

It can be argued that a pendulum is the most underrated tool available to anyone who is seeking clarity and guidance from within. When used properly, it can move your life forward in ways that you may not be able to imagine. Our view is that the simplicity and ease of a pendulum is unmatched by any other tool. It's hard to believe that something so simple can unlock tremendous power within us.

Ancient Origins of the Pendulum

Evidence of pendulum use spans across many cultures dating back thousands of years; however, their actual use may pre-date recorded history. Pendulum use arose from the art and discipline of dowsing, the practice of locating water sources, lost objects, and minerals underground.[14] Pendulums were also used for divination—the practice of seeking knowledge through the unknown or supernatural.

Dowsing

Dowsing originated with the practice of using a pendulum or a dowsing rod and holding it in the dowser's hand.[15] Dowsers walk over land and let pendulums or dowsing rods guide them to water sources or minerals underground. Dowsers have developed their intuition to tune in to the vibrations of water or other minerals. Since water is critical to survival, this was an important skill throughout history and continues to be used today.

How does dowsing for water work? There's a long-standing belief that the vibration transmitted from underground water sources causes the pendulum or the dowsing rod to move in the hands of the dowser. Anyone can learn to dowse. It is a natural skill that can be improved with practice, such as playing sports or learning a musical instrument. Our bodies' natural abilities are picking up on the vibration, not necessarily perceptible through our five senses, which is causing the pendulum or a dowsing rod to move, signaling that what we are seeking has been found. Part mystery and part science, dowsing has withstood the test of time and is still practiced by many today.[16]

The earliest known findings of dowsing have been unearthed in the Sahara desert of Algeria. In 1949, a group of French explorers discovered the Tassili Caves, a massive system of caverns spanning more than 72,000 kilometers (28,000 square miles). Their goal was to find proof of lost civilizations, so stumbling upon prehistoric cave art, including an enormous wall painting of a dowser,

---

14   Lloyd Youngblood, "Dowsing: An Ancient History," American Society of Dowsers, accessed September 21, 2023, https://dowsers.org/dowsing-history/.

15   William Brown, "Science: The Physics of a Dowsing Pendulum," *NewScientist*, October 6, 1990, https://www.newscientist.com/article/mg12817373-200-science-the-physics-of-a-dowsing-pendulum/.

16   Walt Woods, *Letter to Robin*, 10th ed. (Oroville, CA: The Print Shoppe, 2001), https://lettertorobin.files.wordpress.com/2016/06/rbn_10_4_english.pdf.

must have been quite incredible. The extraordinary painting depicts a man encircled by his tribe and searching for water with a dowsing stick. Carbon dating has determined these painting are at least 8,000 years old.[17]

Pendulums in Ancient History

Pendulums can be found in the collections of the Cairo Museum in Egypt, where they were recovered from tombs dating back thousands of years. In addition, etchings depicting pharaohs holding what is thought to be dowsing rods have been discovered on 4,000 year-old Egyptian temples.[18] Author Richard Webster shares that it is believed that the Egyptians used dowsing to determine where to grow crops, and the Egyptian ankh symbol may represent a pendulum or divining rod.[19]

In ancient China, pendulums were used to block negative spirits and determine where their source originated. "There is an etching of Chinese Emperor Yu who ruled China 2500 years ago, and in his hands he holds a rather bulky turn-pronged device that resembles a dowsing device," shares a member of the American Society of Dowsers.[20] Mathematician and engineer Zhang Heng is credited with inventing the first seismometer in 132 CE, which helped China respond quickly to natural disasters. The seismometer was a copper container that contained a pendulum inside and was sensitive to tremors even hundreds of miles away. An earthquake would trigger the pendulum to swing, knocking loose one of eight balls that indicated the direction of the earthquake's location.[21]

Pendulums during the Renaissance and the Age of Discovery

Pendulums were probably most widely popularized by Galileo in the late sixteenth century and early seventeenth century. His work with pendulums began when he observed a chandelier in a cathedral in continuous perpetual motion. Galileo began exploring the functionality of the pendulum as a time-keeping device in the early 1600s. While he was not able to construct a timepiece due

17 Youngblood, "Dowsing: An Ancient History."

18 Youngblood, "Dowsing: An Ancient History."

19 Richard Webster, *Pendulum Magic for Beginners* (St. Paul, MN: Llewellyn Publications, 2002), xv.

20 Youngblood, "Dowsing: An Ancient History."

21 "Zhang Heng," New World Encyclopedia, accessed September 21, 2023, https://www.newworld encyclopedia.org/entry/Zhang_Heng.

to air friction obstacles, his experiments led to the law of the pendulum, which would subsequently be utilized in the construction of clocks.[22]

Following Galileo's findings, Dutch scientist Christiaan Huygens invented the first pendulum clock in 1656. Pendulum clocks were the standard for accurate timekeeping for over 270 years, until the quartz clock was invented in 1927. Scientifically, pendulums have continued to be of great value in designing machines of greater complexity and aiding in our understanding of modern physics.[23]

Pendulums in the Gilded Age and Beyond

Nineteenth-century French physicist Jean Foucault first used what is known as the "Foucault Pendulum" to "demonstrate the rotation of the earth. It was the first satisfactory demonstration of the earth's rotation using a laboratory apparatus rather than astronomical observations." It was on display for many years at the Smithsonian's National Museum of American History.[24]

Pendulums and the Catholic Church

Over many centuries, the Catholic Church has had a complex relationship with the concept of dowsing. During medieval times, the practice of using pendulums for dowsing and divination was shunned and deemed a form of devil worship. But in the 1700s, it became clear to the Catholic Church that pendulums and dowsing rods were effective in locating water and its use made a successful comeback.

Abbé Mermet, a devout Roman Catholic and French rector, is known as the king of dowsers of the early twentieth century. His dowsing work resulted in extensive findings of underground resources. The Vatican often used his radiesthesia (dowsing) expertise in archeological excavations in Rome.[25] Mermet's book *The Principles and Practice of Radiesthesia* has become a classic. Mermet was a big believer in the scientific roots of radiesthesia: "Personally, I must

---

22   John London, "Facts about Pendulums," Sciencing, last modified April 24, 2017, https://sciencing
      .com/uses-pendulums-8541430.html.

23   Rachel Gaal, "June 16, 1657: Christiaan Huygens Patents the First Pendulum Clock," *APS News 26*, no.
      6 (June 2017), https://www.aps.org/publications/apsnews/201706/history.cfm; London, "Facts about
      Pendulums."

24   "Foucault Pendulum," Smithsonian, accessed September 21, 2023, https://www.si.edu/spotlight
      /foucault-pendulum.

25   Abbé Mermet, *The Principles and Practice of Radiesthesia*, trans. Mark Clement (London: Vincent Stuart,
      1959), 15.

make my own position quite clear. I regard Radiesthesia as being purely scientific. If it had not been so, I should have given it up long ago."[26]

Proper dowsing practice, for the highest good of humankind, is what drives the positive outcomes, not the physical object itself. In his book *Earth Radiation*, Käthe Bachler writes, "The dowsing rod and pendulum are physical objects, and thus neutral, which means they are beyond good and evil, as would be a knife or fire or water. It is true however, that the misuses of those instruments could become dangerous. But in the hands of people with integrity, who use the pendulum and the dowsing rod only in the service of their fellow men, the effects are most beneficial."[27]

Pendulums are still used for dowsing today. They have been used by shamans, scientists, midwives, spiritual and cultural leaders, and everyday people alike. Pendulums have also been used by practitioners of nontraditional and holistic medicine to help detect and diagnose illness, identify allergies and intolerances to certain foods, and locate sources of infection.[28] In modern times, pendulums are most commonly used by everyday people like us to help answer questions. These ancient tools have survived the test of time—and they are making a comeback!

Pendulum Basics

Learning to use a pendulum properly is important. Honing your pendulum practice will assist you to receive the most accurate guidance and clarity you seek to move your life forward in a way that is most optimal for you. There is much to learn and it's tough to know where to begin.

Here are a few key points to keep in mind to get you started on your pendulum journey:

1. Pendulums are to be used responsibly and ethically. Sometimes there's information that you are not supposed to know at a certain point in time, or it is simply none of your business.

---

26 Mermet, *The Principles and Practice of Radiesthesia*, 20.

27 Käthe Bachler, *Earth Radiation* (John Living, 2007), 65.

28 John London, "Facts about Pendulums," Sciencing, last modified April 24, 2017, https://sciencing.com/pendulums-8538891.html.

2. Your pendulum practice is truly your own practice. Being respectful about others' privacy is key to ethically using your pendulum. Do not ask questions about other people without their permission. It is optimal to keep your questions focused on yourself. As an example, if you are wondering if someone wants to spend time with you, frame that question in a way that relates to you. For instance, "Is it optimal for me to spend time with Sidney this week?" versus "Does Sidney want to spend time with me this week?"

3. It is important to be open to using a pendulum. If you don't believe that a pendulum can work for you, guess what? It won't. Our beliefs create our reality. Pendulums should be taken seriously and respected. They require practice, patience, and belief.

4. Establishing a close bond and relationship with your pendulum is necessary. A strong connection will increase the effectiveness of the pendulum and how it works with your energy. The connection with your pendulum should be nurtured. We will cover tips on how to do this in chapter 5.

5. Do not ask the pendulum a question when you are feeling emotionally charged. Having strong emotions about the outcome may create bias and result in your pendulum giving you an inaccurate answer. If this is the case, we recommend that you pause working with your pendulum for the moment and resume when you are feeling less emotionally invested in the topic.

6. Pendulums should always be used for your highest good and the highest good of all. They should never be used with harmful or negative intentions. This will not serve you or anyone.

7. Pendulums are not religious tools; they are energetic tools. They can be used by everyone with any belief system. The key is to put aside your doubts and engage in this practice with curiosity, focusing on optimal outcomes for all.

If you are called to go beyond your subconscious for guidance, you can also use your pendulum to connect to your higher self, the all-knowing aspect of you that is connected to universal intelligence (often referred to as God, Source, the Divine, or whatever term resonates most with you). Your higher self has the answers you seek and will provide them to you when you ask for guidance and trust. Think of your higher self as an optimal extension of your intuitive abilities. When connecting to your higher self, you can also invite your spirit guides, guardian angels and any other divine beings of love and light who are supporting you for your optimal outcomes and the optimal outcomes for all.

It is simple to connect to your higher self and any other beings of light and love that you are feeling called to by inviting them to come in when you begin your pendulum session. Then ask if they are present with you and wait for your answer to show up through your pendulum. Our beings of love and light always show up for us when we invite them. They will also show up for you. We will explore your higher self, your angels, spirit guides, and more in chapter 5.

Another incredible benefit of a pendulum is that it can be used to amplify and disseminate energy on a vibrational level far and beyond your own energy field. You can work with your pendulum to disseminate positive thoughts and energy to others who are in need of healing or to send out positive vibes to spread love and peace. You can do this anytime and anywhere with the help of your pendulum. It's easy to do and the world will be better off for it! We witnessed the impact of this firsthand when we organized an event called Peace, Prayers, and Pendulums for Ukraine in March 2022.

STORY: PEACE, PRAYERS, AND PENDULUMS

Sometimes we feel helpless as we witness conflict across the globe. The eruption of war in Ukraine prompted us to create an event focused on spreading peace, prayers, and love across the universe with the help of pendulums. There were prayers, poems, songs, chants, and even a beautiful harp performance. Everyone's words were full of hope, inspiration, and healing—everything that we envisioned when we planned the event. We ended the event surrounding a peace pole in a circle. Together, we let our pendulums swing to expand our collective energy and send out positive energy and healing into the world. Together, we chanted, "Let there be peace, kindness, compassion, community, action, love, freedom, health, strength. Let there be peace." It was truly magical.

Exercise
SPREADING POSITIVE VIBES

The good news about this exercise is that you don't have to be a pendulum expert to do it. In fact, you don't need to know anything about how to use a pendulum to spread positive vibes. If you have a pendulum already, that's great. Let's put it to good use. If not, grab a necklace or hang a weighted object from a string and give this exercise a go.

1. Start out by setting an intention to spread positive thoughts or loving and healing energy or to simply to share love, peace, and happiness throughout the universe.
2. Hold your pendulum at the top of the chain or string and ask it to show you the movement for sending positive energy and healing to the world, others, a specific person, or whomever/whatever you're wanting to impact. The pendulum will show you.
3. Keep holding the pendulum and visualize in your mind's eye whom you'd like to send positive energy or healing to.
4. Let the pendulum begin to move. Your pendulum will begin to swing in the motion that signals positive energy.
5. Continue to visualize positive energy in your mind's eye and feel the joy and vibration in your heart. Imagine your light emanating from inside your body and spreading outward. Imagine spreading your light as far and wide as you'd like.
6. Let the pendulum continue to move as long as it takes. It will settle down and come to a stop when it's ready.
7. Your work is done.

You might feel a tingling sensation and a lightness around you. Whatever you feel, know that you've done amazing and seriously impactful work!

Chapter 3
HOW TO PICK YOUR PENDULUM

Being drawn to pendulums or a particular pendulum is the heart signaling that you are in a place in your life where you are truly ready to begin the journey toward your most optimal outcomes. If you're not making your own pendulum, we have some advice on how to find the perfect one for you.

Whether shopping for a pendulum in person or online, most often, the first pendulum a person is drawn to is the one they end up choosing. Other times, it's trial and error and you'll want to try out several. We have plenty of customers tell us their pendulum just "jumped out" at them. We've learned that more often than not, your pendulum picks you versus the other way around. A pendulum can be ornate or just a piece of metal on a string. Picking a pendulum is similar to picking a crystal or anything else that appeals to you. The most important aspect of selecting a pendulum is having a strong connection with it. You want to love it, as you're going to be using it and bonding with it often.

A few things to consider when choosing a pendulum are what material, weight, and shape you prefer. You can also choose a pendulum based on the purpose of use. Another aspect to think about is how long the chain is, which can vary as well.

It's perfectly okay to use different pendulums for various reasons. We know many who own several (including ourselves). You may want to have one for sharing with others, one to use for energy work, one for work purposes, and one that is strictly personal to you. What's crucial is your connection with the pendulum, so trust your intuition!

Crystals

Many pendulums are made with crystals and gemstones, which hold a high vibration and offer healing and nurturing properties. Plus, they are beautiful and mystical at the same time. These pendulums come in various shapes and sizes. Most of the ones we work with are of a hexagonal shape. That means that they have six cut sides. The hexagonal shape symbolizes harmony and natural order and is often seen in nature, such as in snowflakes and honeycomb. Creating intentional combinations of crystals and gemstones in pendulums enhances the pendulum experience and opens the gateway to inner knowing even further. It's fun to mix and match crystals since each one holds different vibrations and healing energies. For example, if you're wanting to focus on your health, you may want to choose a clear quartz crystal since it is considered a master healer and amplifies all other healing properties. Or if you'd like to bring in the energy of financial freedom, try an amazonite for success and abundance.

Metals

Pendulums can also be crafted with metal or wood. Common metals used are silver, gold, copper, brass, and steel. Pendulums made with metal are very durable and are sometimes preferred by those who use them in a variety of the healing arts. This is because crystals and gemstones absorb energy—yours as well as the energy of those around you. Metal and wood pendulums do not. Metals act as natural conductors of energy from your magnetic field as well as that of the earth's. These pendulums are a bit heavier and thus swing strongly, making it easier to read the answers. You'll often see metal pendulums shaped like an inverted teardrop with a sharp point. Sometimes metal pendulums come with a chamber or small compartment that can be opened and closed. You can include different objects in them to create a specific connection with your pendulum and to help you work on a more specific purpose. Metals are more durable than crystals and are therefore not damaged as easily. Nevertheless, we encourage caring for metal pendulums like those with crystals and gemstones.

Wood

Wood pendulums are lightweight and neutral, making them a great choice for practitioners who use them with others. Wood is another natural energy that is less influenced by the magnetic field and unwanted energy. If you're going to be working with clients or friends to do one-on-one readings for them, you may want to choose a metal or wood pendulum to avoid energetic interference.

Weight and Shape

The weight of the pendulum you work with is a personal preference. As mentioned, metals tend to be heavier; however, it also depends on the size and other materials of the pendulum. The most common shapes for pendulums are teardrop, chambered or Mermet, hexagonal, merkaba, and sephoroton.

A teardrop pendulum is rounded with a fine point at the end. It resembles an inverted teardrop and symbolizes water. One of the most common pendulum shapes, it is often referred to as the beginner's pendulum because it is easy to use and perfect for pendulum beginners. This type of pendulum tends to have an even swing since the teardrop narrows toward the end, while the thicker part is attached to the chain.

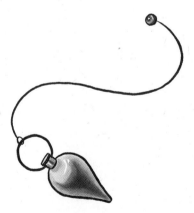

Figure 3: Teardrop pendulum

A chambered pendulum, also known as the Mermet pendulum (named after Abbé Alexis Mermet, who invented this kind of pendulum in the 1930s), contains a very small chamber that can be opened. The purpose of this is to enhance your pendulum practice by placing other items inside, such as herbs, oils, crystals, or a piece of hair belonging to the person who is using it. We often recommend writing down your intention on a small piece of paper and putting it into the chamber of the pendulum. That way, you can amplify the manifestation of your intention with the pendulum's energy.

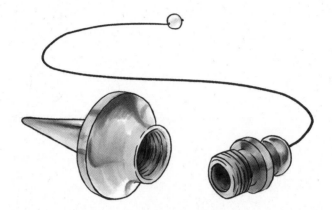

Figure 4: Chambered pendulum

A hexagonal pendulum is often made with crystals, cut on six sides to create a point. A hexagon is nature's most efficient shape and represents balance, harmony, and connection. Hexagons are prevalent in nature due to their efficiency. It uses the least amount of material to hold the most weight, making it an ideal shape for any type of pendulum practice.

Figure 5: Hexagon pendulum

The merkaba-shaped pendulum has a special meaning and purpose. The merkaba is a sacred shape from Jewish mysticism that is believed to have powerful spiritual properties that may help us reach higher states of consciousness. This symbol is created when two tetrahedrons are combined, one pointing up to the heavens, channeling energy down from the universe to Earth, and one pointing down, drawing energy up from Earth. *Mer* means "light," *Ka* means "spirit," and *Ba* means "body."[29]

Figure 6: Merkaba pendulum

A sephoroton pendulum typically has a crystal or gemstone sphere and a metal tip. This perfectly balanced shape has given this pendulum a reputation of being extremely reliable. Since it radiates energy from all angles, it is highly sensitive to vibrations and is perfect for beginners and experienced pendulum users.

Figure 7: Sephoroton pendulum

29 "Merkaba Symbol," Ancient-Symbols.com, accessed November 6, 2023, https://www.ancient-symbols.com/symbols-directory/merkaba.html.

Chain Length

Some pendulums are longer than others, and again, it boils down to personal preference. There are various schools of thought on how long a pendulum should be. Typically, the chain of a pendulum will be approximately six to eight inches long. For some, a shorter chain is easier to work with, and for others, it's the opposite. When choosing a pendulum, see how the chain feels in relation to the entirety of the pendulum. How does it swing for you? Is it comfortable to hold in your hand? There's no right or wrong.

Basic Pendulum-Making Ideas

Whether you choose to purchase a pendulum or make one yourself, the most important factor is that you made a choice to work with one. As mentioned, anything weighted on a string can be a pendulum, and designs can range from very simple to highly complex and artistic. If you choose to make your own, the main ingredient you need is your imagination and you'll be well on your way. Below are some ideas to get you started.

- Use any existing necklace with a pendant.
- Try attaching a paperclip to the end of a string.
- Attach a chain or leather string to your favorite ring. You may want to use an old family heirloom or a piece that holds sentimental value for you. Doing so can enhance your connection with it.
- Find an old key and attach it to a string or a chain through the hole on top.
- Use an old pocket watch with a chain if you have one around.
- Take a look at what's sitting in your jewelry box that you can repurpose into a pendulum.
- You can also make a pendulum out of many small household objects made of just about any material, like wood, metal, or stone. Have fun and experiment, and the right pendulum will come together.

Pendulum Buying Tips

If you decide to purchase a pendulum, we have lots of tips for you. Whether you're buying a pendulum at a metaphysical store or a craft fair, we encourage you to make this an interactive experience. When a certain pendulum catches your eye, here are a few things you should consider:

- Hold the pendulum in your hands and notice how you feel. Does it feel good? Do you get any kind of tingling sensation? Is there a change in your body temperature? Where do you feel it in your body? Listen to your intuition and your body.

- Hold it in your dominant hand and notice if it moves in your hand. If it does, that's a good indication that you're connecting with that pendulum.

- If it doesn't move and stays completely still, that one might not be the right one for you at this time. This doesn't mean that particular pendulum won't *ever* work for you, but it is possible that there is a better choice for you.

- Trying several pendulums is perfectly okay. In fact, we encourage you to try as many as you'd like. We've had customers who have tried nearly thirty pendulums in one sitting!

- When choosing a pendulum, a surefire way to know if it's the right pendulum for you is to simply ask it. After calibrating the pendulum and determining your yes and no movements (discussed in chapter 4), ask, "Is the pendulum that I'm currently holding the right pendulum for me?" You'll get a clear yes or no. If you're trying to decide between two or three pendulums, hold each one and ask, "Is the pendulum that I am holding the *most* optimal pendulum for me at this time?"

- When considering purchasing a crystal pendulum, understanding the healing properties of the crystals is another way to help you make your selection. If you're trying to manifest something specific in your life, look for a crystal with attributes that can assist you.

- When you believe that you've found *the* pendulum, notice how you feel about it. Do you feel calm, peaceful, joyful,

happy, or excited? Does your hand tingle when you're holding the pendulum?

- If you did not purchase the pendulum and keep thinking
  about it, it's probably the right pendulum for you. It's calling you because you have made a magical connection with
  it. Trust your intuition and go back and get it. We have seen
  this scenario play out many times with our customers. They
  leave and come back to buy their perfect pendulum because
  it kept calling out to them.

- It's possible to select a pendulum as a gift as well. Calibrate
  the pendulum you picked to find your yes and no and ask it
  if it's the right pendulum for your intended recipient. Your
  intuition will guide you through this process. And have faith
  that the right pendulum will find its perfect owner. It always
  does somehow.

- Shopping for a pendulum online is similar to an in-person
  experience, minus the ability to touch and feel the crystals.
  Look at what you're drawn to and trust your instincts.

One thing we've learned about picking a pendulum is that if you're meant
to have a specific pendulum, you will. We have countless stories about how
customers have found their pendulums synchronistically. Trust the process and
believe!

One of our favorite examples of this occurred very early in our pendulum
journey. We were just getting started. We had brought in our pendulums to
show to the owner of a local metaphysical boutique. While we were showing
the pendulums and talking with the staff, a customer who happened to be in
the shop couldn't help but notice a particular pendulum with a sparkling star
that she was immediately drawn to. At that time, it wasn't for sale. We went on
with our meeting and decided that we would hold a pop-up trunk show for the
holidays at the boutique. We were so excited, as this was one of our first opportunities to showcase our pendulums to the world! About three weeks later, we
were at the store again to prepare for the trunk show. Well, synchronistically,
the same customer happened to be there, and we had the sparkling star pendulum she fell in love with on hand. She ended up purchasing the pendulum that

she had been drawn to weeks before. That pendulum was clearly meant to be hers and found its way to her.

Another occurrence we will never forget is from an event we were at in Austin, Minnesota. A woman who was so drawn to a certain pendulum couldn't decide if she should purchase it. We don't "try" to sell our pendulums. They sell themselves and synchronistically find the right hands they're meant to be with. So she left our table without the pendulum. Later that day, she reappeared. She was overjoyed that the pendulum she was drawn to was still there and revealed that she had left the event and driven over thirty miles, only to turn around and come back for it. She said she couldn't stop thinking about it!

Picking out a pendulum is all about having fun with the process. At the core, we encourage you to trust your intuition. Remember that there is no right or wrong so go with your gut. Follow the tips on the previous pages and trust yourself. After connecting thousands of people with their most optimal pendulums, we strongly believe that the right pendulum finds its rightful owner. Whether you choose your pendulum, it chooses you, or you are gifted one, it's more about the heart-centered connection that you establish with it.

SUZIE'S STORY

I met Lana and Karina when they enthusiastically, and perhaps nervously, walked into my art gallery in Minneapolis. They kindly asked if I had time to look at their handcrafted line of pendulum jewelry. My initial thought was that they were new artists looking for a place to sell a few pieces, nothing more. However, within a couple of minutes I was drawn to their energy. There was something about Lana and Karina that I was immediately drawn to. Good vibes. They asked me if I knew anything about pendulums. I of course said yes. Truth is, the extent of my knowledge goes back to my teen years when some of my girlfriends would gather for the "string test." We would tie a penny or washer or something similar to the end of a string. We would then proceed to ask a string of important questions, like "Does Johnny Miller like me?" The string would swing one way for yes and another way for no. Seemed like a good way to find out the answer to important questions and decision-making.

Over the years, I have searched, studied, and explored various energetic modalities, so I was intrigued with Lana and Karina standing in front of me and sharing their knowledge. We played with a few of the pendulums, and

> *I thought I knew which piece I would like to have as mine. Through more exper-imentation and asking it questions, I knew I needed to get my head out of the way, open my heart, and let the pendulum choose me. Through Lana and Kar-ina's guidance, I learned to trust the Divine and use the pendulum as a tool for balance and spiritual awareness. We are all energy, and if we allow ourselves to open up that energy and transfer it to the vibration of the pendulum, we will be guided to find the Divine within.*
>
> *There was no doubt that I wanted to carry their beautiful pendulums at the gallery, host events with them, support their mission, and be friends with them. We laugh now about how we were divinely brought together. When asked about collaborating with HeartCentric, my pendulum gave a strong yes!*

Pendulums with Healing Crystals and Gemstones

Since the majority of the pendulums we work with are crafted with high-vibration crystals and gemstones, we thought we'd share more information about their properties. Crystals hold energetic and healing properties that can be harnessed to help you in your everyday life. Incorporate them into pendulums, and their power is amplified. Crystals and stones are as old as the earth itself and for centuries have been prized for their beauty and as symbols of power. In many ancient cultures, their sacred meaning and healing properties were just as important as their ability to dazzle.

Crystals harness vibrations of light. As they absorb and alchemize energy, our bodies also take in their electromagnetic frequencies. This process can be thought of as crystals speaking to our cells, which is why they often make us feel better. When you hold a crystal, you're holding a piece of history. Today, they are used not only for their healing benefits but also for modern tools and electronics such as lasers, inkjet printers, quartz watches, microphones, sonar, and medical implants.[30]

"Gemstones and crystals…absorb, store, reflect and radiate light in the form of intelligent fields of stable energy that increase the flow of vital life force within the human physical body and subtle body," writes energy healer Hazel Raven.[31] Various crystals are believed to act as conduits for healing, enabling pos-

---

30   Meg Walters, "Healing Crystals: What They Can and Can't Do," Healthline, July 20, 2023, https://www.healthline.com/health/healing-crystals-what-they-can-do-and-what-they-cant.

31   Hazel Raven, *The Angel Bible* (New York: Sterling Publishing, 2006), 280.

itive energy to flow into the body as negative energy flows out. Oriental Healing and Oasis and Wellness Center describes the philosophy of modern crystal healing as being "based on traditional concepts borrowed from Asian cultures, most notably the Chinese concept of life-energy (chi or qi) and the Hindu or Buddhist concept of chakras, which are vortices of life-energy that connect the physical and supernatural elements of the body."[32] (This will be discussed more in chapter 6.) Crystals have a high vibration that raises consciousness and opens our minds to other realms. These stones are helping shape human beings in the New Earth and accelerate evolution on Earth. Here are some of our favorite crystals to work with:

Amethyst

Amethyst is a powerful crystal for a variety of intentions. This calming stone allows you to quiet your mind, which can help move you through life from a higher state of being. Amethyst can aid in deepening your connection to yourself and strengthen your intuitive abilities. Besides facilitating your intuitive sense, amethyst may also help you work toward inner peace and balance and allow you to relax when you need to most, such as before bed, during a stressful situation, or during meditation.

Aventurine

Aventurine, especially green aventurine, is a soothing and calming stone that helps with overall well-being. It encourages empathy and compassion while helping with decision-making. We enjoy working with green aventurine because it can be a helpful stone for an individual to take action on the guidance they receive from their intuition while working with their pendulum. Aventurine is also known to bring together emotions and intellect, creating a smoother path for our journey and dissolving any cognitive dissonance that we may experience. Prosperity, positivity, and perseverance are also important and valuable attributes that green aventurine helps promote. When working with aventurine, keep your heart open and be on the lookout for the gifts to come.

---

32 "Crystal & Gemstone Therapy," Oriental Healing Oasis and Wellness Center, accessed September 22, 2023.

Citrine

Citrine brings forth sun energy to light up all areas of your life. Keeping this stone close will help you keep your energy light and bright. When you are filled with positive energy, you can more easily connect to your inner light, as well as bring a sense of joy, happiness, and optimism to all areas of your life. Citrine may help you increase your personal power and self-confidence as well as dissolve any stagnation, resulting in higher energy levels. Citrine is ideal for a variety of intentions, including happiness, confidence, manifestation, prosperity, generosity, and creativity.

Fluorite

Fluorite is a crystal that comes in many colors, including blue, green, purple, yellow, and brown. Oftentimes, fluorite has beautiful properties of multiple colors and is referred to as rainbow fluorite. It is a purifying and cleansing crystal that keeps any negative energy away. Fluorite can help us overcome chaos that we may be experiencing on a daily basis and bring structure and organization to our lives. Fluorite is extremely helpful with decision-making because it helps us stay rooted in truth and clarity. When your pendulum work guides you toward your truth, fluorite helps you take appropriate action.

Hematite

Hematite is known to help with focus, confidence, optimism, balance, and energetic protection. It is a grounding stone that also enhances willpower and reliability. Hematite is also very helpful in strengthening memory and stimulating concentration. It also highlights missed opportunities and unfulfilled wants and desires. This is a wonderful stone for students of all ages because it helps develop the confidence to achieve while stimulating focus.

Jasper

Jasper is a beautiful stone that comes in many varieties and colors. It is known to help align our mental, physical, and emotional bodies. Jasper, like aventurine, can help bring us courage to take action on our decisions. Jasper is also good for letting go of the past. It guides us to take an honest look at ourselves and open up to healing those parts that we may have neglected. Jasper plays a part in bringing our visions to life while stimulating our creativity and imagination.

Labradorite

Labradorite is a very protective stone that shields us from the negativity of the world as well as the negativity within ourselves. This stone helps us dig deep within ourselves and bring to the surface our suppressed emotions and memories. Labradorite stimulates our spiritual gifts and psychic abilities while helping us raise our consciousness. Additionally, labradorite is helpful in breaking unhealthy patterns such as addictions because it attracts strength and resilience when we are facing challenges.

Lapis Lazuli

Lapis lazuli sharpens our intuition, wisdom, and spiritual growth. It also helps with communication and encourages clear expression when sharing information. Lapis lazuli supports learning because it aids in improving memory and the ability to process information. Carrying or wearing lapis lazuli can help you release stress and bring in a sense of inner peace. It can also aid in increasing creativity and adding clarity to your life.

Obsidian

Obsidian comes in a variety of colors, including black, blue, brown, green, and several others. Our favorite is black obsidian. It is made from molten lava that has no time to crystallize. Black obsidian is highly protective. It dispels negativity and supports us through change. It is helpful in discarding false beliefs and surfacing the truth. Black obsidian is very grounding and teaches us to use our power for the greatest good of all.

Pyrite

Pyrite is a great stone to work with when manifesting abundance, confidence, and protection. It's known as fool's gold because its color and luster caused people to mistake it for gold. The name *pyrite* comes from the Greek word for "fire," and it creates sparks when struck. Pyrite shields, protects, and may even help make thoughtful business decisions. Pyrite is also a great manifestation stone. When you manifest with pyrite, we recommend that you state what it is you're trying to manifest out loud. Hearing yourself say what you want helps you see that it really is very achievable.

Quartz

There are many types of quartz, but the one we work with most often is clear quartz. It is a high-vibration crystal that helps us clear our mind, body, and spirit and align ourselves with a path of our highest potential. Quartz is also a powerful amplifier because of its helical spiral crystalline form. We like crystal quartz because it is helpful in manifesting our intentions. It is useful for a variety of intentions, such as manifesting abundance, promoting peace and calm, and clearing out stagnant energy. Quartz is also wonderful at the office because it promotes concentration and memory and calms an overactive mind.

Rose Quartz

Rose quartz is most known for attracting love and partnership. Going beyond romantic love, rose quartz is also strongly linked with compassion and unconditional love, making it an ideal crystal for relationships. Rose quartz may help enhance kindness for yourself, loved ones, and all living things. It's also great for attracting a new relationship and strengthening an existing partnership. Rose quartz helps open the heart and restores trust. If you have been holding on to negativity from the past, rose quartz may help you replace those feelings with thoughts of unconditional love and accept past situations in order to transform them into a state of a higher vibration.

Tiger's Eye

Tiger's eye is a very practical stone that helps us decipher what we want from what we need. It is also helpful when we need to separate our own needs from the needs of others. Tiger's eye encourages us to seek answers from within, rather than the outside world, which makes it a powerful component for pendulums. It also prompts us to take practical and useful action on the guidance that we receive from pendulum work.

Crystals are powerful beings themselves and need to be treated with respect. They absorb and transmit energy efficiently, and as such, they should be cleansed and charged on a regular basis to keep them functioning properly. Energy exchange is vital between you and your crystals, so treat them with respect, and they will show you how they can be used to enhance your life and overall well-being.

Here's a story from a customer and now a friend who found not one but two pendulums for her journey.

ASHLEY'S STORY

I met Lana and Karina at an event hosted by The Edge *magazine and was instantly drawn to a pendulum (Mystic Crystal) that was used as an example while we were at the event.*

After being given direction on how to use it, I was immediately able to find my yes and no swings, dove straight in, and started asking questions (inside my head). The pendulum swung differently depending on what I asked it, and the answers just felt right to me.

A few months later, I had another conversation with Lana and Karina to chat about working together and was drawn to yet another pendulum (Sanctuary Shell) that they had with them. I knew the moment I saw it that I had to have it—it has an opalite crystal and a moonstone, two of my favorites, and is absolutely beautiful. I use this pendulum whenever I'm feeling anxious about something or want to know if I'm on the right track for myself when it comes to my career, family, and other things in life. So far, it has yet to steer me in the wrong direction. I'm truly grateful I was able to meet these wonderful women, who have shown me the power of the pendulum! Not just in my personal life, but also in my professional life and beyond. I've even gotten to share this knowledge with friends who were interested!

Chapter 4
CARING FOR AND USING YOUR PENDULUM

So you've found the perfect pendulum for you. Whether it's a pendulum that you purchased, one that was gifted to you, or one that you made yourself, this remarkable tool has found the right hands—yours! Maybe you bonded with your pendulum right away. Or perhaps you were drawn to your pendulum for a reason you're still unclear about. We call this divine guidance.

Your pendulum is a personal tool. As such, one of the keys to working with your pendulum is to strengthen your connection with it. Try carrying the pendulum with you for a couple of days so that it can further connect with your energy. You can also sleep with it underneath your pillow. Whatever you decide, keep it close to you for a few days. Over time, you're going to develop a stronger tie with your pendulum as it works with your energy. Since we are both obsessed with pendulums, we love having easy access to them. There's always one in our purses, on our desks, on our nightstands, and in our cars (in case we need to pull over and ask something). Just don't use it while driving. Safety first!

When the pendulum is in your hands and you're using it for the most optimal outcomes for you and for all, you really become an unstoppable force. Our bodies are communicating with us constantly. If you pause to listen and create a dialogue with yourself, you'll begin to develop the most important relationship of your life—your relationship to self.

Calibrating Your Pendulum

Whether you need a quick answer or are sitting down for a lengthier session with your pendulum, we suggest calibrating your pendulum each time you use it. This is easy to do. Remember, a pendulum will give you yes, no, maybe, and not now answers. But first, you have to understand what your individual yes, no, maybe, and not now motions are. The ways in which the pendulum moves are specific to you and will be different from others. Here's a step-by-step guide to getting started:

1. Get yourself grounded and determine the source of where you would like your answers to come from. If you do not specify a source for answers, you will receive your answers from your subconscious. If you'd like to connect with the spiritual realm, you may invite your higher self—the part of you that is connected to universal intelligence and has access to information beyond what your conscious mind is able to process. Additionally, if you are called to do so, you may invite your spirit guides, your guardian angels, archangels, ascended masters, or any other beings of love and light that you connect with.

2. Next comes a crucial step of setting an intention for each session. Establish what you want to get clarity around. Say it aloud or write it down. Let go of any preconceived notions, stay open to the guidance that shows up, and trust the answers that you are about to receive.

3. Hold the top of your pendulum (opposite end of the pointed crystal, wood, or metal bottom) using the thumb and index finger of your dominant hand. You can place your other hand underneath the pendulum to steady the energy flow. Hold the pendulum away from your body by extending your arm if you can. Elbow to fingertips is fine. This ensures that your auric field and energy won't interfere with the answers.

4. Ask your pendulum to show you a yes motion. You can say out loud, "Dear universe (angels, spirit guides, whatever or whoever you feel called to), please show me a yes motion." Watch what direction and motion your pendulum swings. This is your individual and personal yes motion. Note that you don't have to ask your questions out loud. Thinking the question will work just as well.

5. Now do the same to find out what your no motion looks like: "Dear universe, please show me a no motion." And do the same to learn what your maybe and not now motions are. Maybe and not now motions let you know that you may not be ready to receive information at this point in time.

Once you're clear on your individual movements, your pendulum is calibrated and you can begin working with it. Honing your intuitive abilities can take time and patience. Some find it easy to focus and connect right away, while others need more time. Don't worry if your pendulum isn't swinging wildly. The pendulum moves differently for everyone, meaning some people experience really large pendulum swings, and for others, their movement is gentler. Over time and with practice, your pendulum will be swaying like a kid on a merry-go-round!

Most importantly, have fun. Pendulums can truly delight and fuel your soul. Looking inward for validation versus seeking information from external sources will always lead you down the right path. After all, knowing that *you* are the one answering your own questions is the most empowering and authentic way to live.

Cleansing and Caring for Your Pendulum

Many pendulums are made with crystals and gemstones and likened to a piece of personal jewelry. We recommend that you care for them as such. As you create a bond with yours, it will become sentimental. Since you'll be spending many moments with your pendulum, taking good care of it will ensure that it's working optimally with your energy. It's important to cleanse and charge your pendulum regularly just as you would your other crystals and gemstones. Over time, natural stones and crystals pick up and store both positive and negative energies. Most of the time, the energy stored in your pendulum is very beneficial. The key is setting positive intentions for your highest good. However, if there is any negativity or old energy that has accumulated in the crystals, it can inhibit the pendulum's effectiveness.

On a rare occasion when a person tries to use a pendulum, they may find that it does not react as actively as they'd like, or not at all. There are several reasons this can happen, but don't fret. One reason is that you probably have to spend more time connecting and bonding with your pendulum. Another good possibility is that it has been handled by others and has absorbed their energies. A little bit of cleansing and charging should take care of that.

Even if your pendulum doesn't contain crystals, you still want to enhance your pendulum work by taking good care of it. So how do you care for your pendulum? There are various approaches and methods to keep your pendulum charged and free of stagnant energy. Here are some of our favorites.

Selenite

We use selenite more than any other method. Selenite is a raw, white stone that has purifying and cleansing properties. It has a very high vibration and strong healing properties that help clear blocked energy and elevate the spirit. Simply place the crystals of your pendulum on top of or next to a slab of selenite so that they are touching for a period of time. We recommend at least an hour or two, but overnight is most optimal. Even though selenite is perfect to cleanse and purify crystal and gemstone pendulums, it occasionally needs to be cleared and cleansed as well. A good time to cleanse selenite is when you first bring it home, and then on occasion to help wake up its healing potential. We recommend clearing selenite by smoke cleansing. Avoid submerging selenite in water since it's a very soft stone and can dissolve.

Smoke Cleansing

Smoke cleansing is an ancient practice that involves the burning of aromatic plants, resins, wood, and the like for health or spiritual purposes. It is common in a wide variety of cultures and faiths around the world. For smoke cleansing, we recommend that you purchase a consciously sourced herb bundle. We like to use bundles that contain lavender, cedar, rosemary, mint, pine, or lemon balm, since these are sustainable plants. Burn your herb bundle over your pendulum to cleanse it while setting your intentions, saying a blessing, or reciting a prayer or mantra.

Before we take our pendulums on the road, we infuse them with loving energy, set intentions for them to find their rightful owners, and cleanse them with some smoke. We always infuse them with the highest vibrations and positive energy. This is such a beautiful and meaningful practice for us. You can do the same with your pendulum, and we highly recommend it.

Sun and Moon Bathing

Leave your pendulum to charge in the sun for a few hours. This will energize it with high vibrations. Morning or late sun is less intense than the noon time frame. Be careful not to leave it in the sun for more than a few hours, as this may fade and damage certain crystals, such as amethyst or fluorite. Unlike sunlight, moonlight is safe for all stones. Let your pendulum sit outside or on a windowsill and absorb the moonlight for a good, deep cleanse and charge. This is a great method to use, especially during a full moon.

Visualizing a Cleansing Light

Visualization is a great tool to cleanse, restore balance, and provide an immediate sense of peace and relaxation to any part of your life. It also works well with pendulums. Hold your pendulum in your hands or close to your heart. You can also place it in front of you on a surface. Visualize a beautiful, healing white light surrounding the pendulum and washing through it and cleansing it. Continue to hold space for your pendulum until you feel your energy shift to a clearer, more purified state.

Methods We Do Not Recommend for Cleansing or Charging

We do not recommend burying your pendulum in soil, using salt, or bathing it in water. While these can be great practices for other materials, water and salt especially can damage and corrode the stones and crystals and cause chipping or breakage.

Charging Your Pendulum

After your pendulum is cleansed, you'll want to recharge it. Recharging puts beneficial positive energy back into the stones. To charge, you can use more blessings or even your own physical touch. You can also use therapeutic sound, such as singing bowls, and visualization.

Below is a short blessing we like to use. We invite you to adapt the words to what feels right for you.

I charge this pendulum with love and light. May it bring me the wisdom, inner guidance, and joy that I seek. I send my pendulum the most positive energy for optimal outcomes, for my highest good and the highest good of all. Thank you, thank you, thank you.

By taking good care of your pendulum, you'll ensure a long and healthy bond with it and, more importantly, with yourself.

Storing and Carrying Your Pendulum

When your pendulum is not in use, the best way to store it at home is to rest it on a piece of selenite, similar to the cleansing method described earlier.

Your pendulum is the ultimate companion, always offering the best advice anytime and anywhere you need it. Remember, it's your amazing guidance assistant (AGA). As such, we recommend that you carry your pendulum with you everywhere that you go. You'll want to make sure that your pendulum has a nice carrying pouch or case that will protect it. Any material that is soft will do. Since you'll be on the go with your pendulum, we also recommend that you include a smaller piece of selenite in your pouch if your pendulum is made of sturdy materials. That way, your pendulum will always remain cleansed of any external energy that isn't wanted, and it will remain charged and ready to assist you the moment that you need it. Selenite is a soft stone, and while we have never had any issues with breakage, we suggest using your best judgment, especially if your pendulum is fragile.

Creating a Sacred Space for Working with Your Pendulum

Find a quiet space in your home where you will not be constantly disturbed by others. Ideally, we recommend that this space has a door you can close, but any space you can claim for a period of time will do. We encourage you to be free from distractions. Your space can have some pillows or cushions to sit on or a desk if that's more comfortable for you. Avoid bringing your cell phone, computer, or other technology into this area if you can, as tech gadgets emit electromagnetic frequencies, which may interfere with your pendulum work.

Add some candles and crystals to this sacred space. Smoke cleanse your space to enhance the energy. Bring in other objects that you're drawn to, such as

Himalayan salt lamps, essential oils, artwork, plants, windchimes, books, tarot decks, oracle cards, and anything else that brings joy, peace, and calm to your heart. If you're partial to sound, play some meditation music, singing bowls, chimes, or any other sound that helps you get grounded. Keep water nearby to ensure that you are always hydrated when doing your pendulum work.

Your sacred space does not need to be indoors. If you have a quiet space in your yard where you can connect with nature, bringing your pendulum practice outdoors is also a good idea. You can even try your local park, a beach, a garden, or any other outdoor space that is quiet and peaceful.

How to Use a Pendulum for Optimal Results

One thing we learned early on in our pendulum journey is that you really *can* use a pendulum on a daily basis to tap into your intuition for multiple uses. A pendulum is a wonderful companion to help you navigate your life. You can think of it as your eyes and ears when you need help making decisions. It's your personal amazing guidance assistant! When using a pendulum, let go of any attachment to the outcome and allow the answer that will serve all involved to show up. This involves releasing any personal attachment to "being right" by letting the ego step aside.

When beginning your pendulum journey, follow these basic guidelines:

Ease into Your Pendulum Practice

How to use a pendulum can be learned quickly, and it's simple for anyone. However, like anything to be mastered, it takes practice to hone your skill. Start slow and allow yourself the time to get comfortable with your pendulum. You may be eager to dive right in and inquire about major life decisions—"Is it optimal for me to change careers at this time?" We advise you to begin with smaller, less consequential questions. Take your time to get very familiar with your pendulum before delving into serious life decisions. Once you learn how to ask the right questions, you'll develop more confidence in accessing your intuitive guidance. This will empower you to start taking action on the information you're getting and seeing great results. You'll then be prepared to dive into deeper, more high-stakes questions.

Take Notice of the Results You're Getting

With time, you will notice yourself getting more and more comfortable working with your pendulum and learning to trust what your intuition is telling you. You'll begin to rely on your intuition as an ongoing companion and guide through your daily journey. Keep reminding yourself to check in with your intuition throughout the day. When you're regularly accessing your intuition with your pendulum, don't forget to take a moment to reflect on what's happening around you. How has the outcome of the choice that your intuition guided you toward impacted you? For example, take notice if the extra work project your intuition guided you to take on resulted in a better relationship with your coworkers or boss. Reflect on whether or not the movie you chose to watch with the whole family led to an enjoyable experience and special moments of connection. Maybe the restaurant that you decided to have dinner at led you to bump into friends you haven't seen in a long time. Just remember, every choice, no matter how big or small, takes us on a path toward opportunities for growth and learning.

Besides the learning and growth, reflecting allows us to turn off autopilot and bring ourselves into the present moment. Pausing and reflecting allows us to stop and smell the roses. Also, remember that you are tapping into the present moment. The pendulum does not predict the future unless you're using it for divination, which we will discuss in chapter 5. Our guidance is to use the pendulum to interpret and clarify what is the most optimal choice for you at this current point in time. You will get the answer you seek about the present moment. Situations and circumstances may change, and if you ask the same question a week later, it is possible to get a different answer. The reason is that you now have more information than you did a week ago. Always remember to keep your questions focused on the present moment and know that the information you receive is one data point in time.

Keep Your Pendulum to Yourself

As you begin getting fabulous results from your pendulum work, your friends and family will take notice. Your confidence and outlook on life will continuously get more positive as you form a deeper connection to your inner wisdom. You might be asked to share your pendulum with others. If you're inclined to show others how a pendulum works and what you currently use it for, that's great. We appreciate you spreading the word about this amazing tool. That said, your personal pendulum is only for you. Its effectiveness will depend on the bond that you establish between you and your pendulum. It will also absorb your energy. For these reasons, we don't recommend sharing a pendulum, as this could cause confusion and result in inaccurate responses for both you and others. If you want to let a friend try it, it's fine to do so for a quick tutorial. Always cleanse and charge the pendulum after others have used it so that any leftover energy that isn't yours is removed. This is very important. If your friends want to learn more, encourage them to pick out their own pendulum and keep educating them about its proper use and care.

Abandon Any Bias or Expectations

Stay open to any and all information you may receive. Start from a place of surrender and release any egoic desires, control, and emotional investment. If you believe that you may be very invested in receiving a certain answer, step away from your practice and come back at a later time when you can approach this work with more clarity and objectivity. To get the most out of your pendulum work, it is imperative that we get out of our own way and be willing to receive answers that will lead to optimal outcomes. Your mind is very powerful. If you want the answer to be yes and are attached to the outcome, it's highly likely that you will sway the answer to be yes. One trick you can try is to close your eyes when you are asking the question. Don't look at the pendulum and let it show you the answer. Once it begins to move, open your eyes and look at the motion. This can help you detach from the answer.

It's important to understand that working with a pendulum is a learned skill and will take practice and dedication. Once you've mastered the basics, there are many ways to hone your pendulum practice. Learning how to trust yourself and discern what is right for you can also have a great impact on those around you. The positive results will benefit you and will have a ripple effect on others.

How to Frame Your Questions

Make sure you ask questions that can be answered with a yes or no. Using an open-ended question will always lead to confusion and an inaccurate response (unless you're using a chart—see page 133). Be specific when you can. Narrow in on your focus by using locations, dates, times, and names. For example, "Is it in my most optimal interest to bring a date to Rebecca's wedding in Colorado on June 10th of this year?"

Ask several simple questions versus one large, complex question. For example, you are creating confusion if you ask, "Is it optimal for me to order a burger or pizza?" Take your time and only ask one yes or no question at a time, such as, "Is it optimal for me to order a burger?" If you get a no, go ahead and ask about the pizza.

The responses you'll receive will be more accurate this way. Ask for a stronger response if needed. Try saying, "Show me a stronger yes (or no)." When phrasing your questions, make sure that you focus on the positive rather than the negative and do not formulate questions that stem from any negative emotions, such as anger or jealousy. For example, instead of asking, "Is this person a negative influence on me?" ask, "Is it optimal for me to spend time with this person?" Stay curious, unattached to the answer, and emotionally neutral. That is the way to get the most accurate and objective results.

When beginning to work with your pendulum, pay attention to what you're thinking. It's normal for your mind to wander. If this happens, start again, as your pendulum will pick up on what you're thinking. This is why it's important to get grounded and stay objective when working with your pendulum. Remember to focus on your session. Be present and don't try to multitask. Stay open-minded and try to remain unbiased about the answers you're going to receive. This may take some practice at first. As tempting as it might be to allow your conscious mind to sway your answers, the answers that you'll receive may not be accurate, which defeats the purpose of the exercise.

Here are some examples of how to word your questions:

- Is it for my most optimal good to [fill in the blank]?
- Is it in the highest good for all concerned to [fill in the blank]?

- Is it optimal for me to believe that it's in my best interest if I [fill in the blank]?
- Would it be ideal for me to [fill in the blank]?
- Am I correct in believing that [fill in the blank]?
- Is it worthwhile for me to [fill in the blank]?

Here are some phrases to avoid:

- "Can I ... ?" We don't know, can you? Your thoughts are very powerful. Believing you can or can't achieve something makes it true. Starting questions with "Can I" may not give you a correct answer. Instead, say, "Is it worthwhile for me to ... ?"
- "Do I need to ... ?" Usually, beyond our basic needs, we don't *need* to have or do anything. Instead, try asking, "Is it in my most optimal good to ... ?"
- "Should I ... ?" This is a vague way to ask a question and is subjective. Instead, ask, "Is it ideal for me to ... ?" Or "Is it in my highest interest to ... ?"

Here's an example of a poorly phrased question: "Should I go to college?" What's wrong with this question? Phrasing your question with "should" leaves room for much interpretation. It's vague and requires you to form an opinion rather than staying objective. A better way to frame this question is this: "Is it in my best interest to go to [college] in [city, state] to study [major] starting in [year or month]?"

If you can't get specific with your questions, you may need to start by asking broad questions and narrowing down your focus based on the answers you're getting. Sometimes we witness people wanting to get specific right away, when in reality, it would be more beneficial to start by casting a wider net. For example, while Karina was watching her niece use her pendulum to find her lost headphones, she instantly started asking if they were in her jacket pocket. Karina encouraged her to start broader and ask the following:

- Are the headphones in my house? *Yes.*
- Are the headphones on the second level of my house? *No.*

- Are the headphones on the main level of my house? *Yes.*
- Are the headphones in the kitchen? *No.*
- Are the headphones in the family room? *No.*
- Are the headphones in the mudroom closet? *Yes.*
- Are the headphones in my black jacket? *No.*
- Are the headphones in my blue jacket? *No.*
- Are the headphones in my red leather purse? *Yes.*

She had forgotten that she left her headphones in her red leather purse last time she used it. Her subconscious mind retained the memory. By being patient with herself and taking time to tap into her wisdom, she was able to quickly narrow down her options with the help of her pendulum, resulting in success. The lesson of this story is to start broad and gradually narrow in as you eliminate your options. You'll achieve greater success by staying calm, patient and connected to your inner wisdom.

Sometimes, you're not meant to know the answer at a certain moment. That is why we recommend programming your pendulum to learn your yes, no, maybe, and not now movements. When you ask a question and the pendulum responds with a not now movement, respect it and move on. You can ask the same question down the road, and if you are meant to know the answer, you will get it.

Knowing When Not to Use Your Pendulum

When it's difficult to stay grounded and objective, your answers may not reflect your true feelings and desires. Thus, starting a pendulum session when you're emotionally charged may throw your answers off. Try to set aside what you don't need and come back to the pendulum when you're in a calmer frame of mind.

There are some occasions when it might be best to put your pendulum on its charging station and let it rest while you ground yourself. This is very positive since you're acknowledging that your energetic state may not be at its most optimal level to go inward. If this happens to you, know that you are practicing self-awareness. Your heart and mind connection can affect the way the pendulum moves, so practice self-care and revisit your questions when you're feeling clear and free.

The following instances may reflect those times when using your pendulum may not be wise.

- You have strong preconceived thoughts about the subject.
- You're feeling intense emotions about the topic you wish to explore.
- You know that you want the answer to be yes or no to a specific question.
- You have fear, anxiety, or strong judgment around a question.
- You're ill, exhausted, or not feeling well.

A good way to test whether you're in the right frame of mind to work with your pendulum is to start with a few basic questions similar to those used when you first calibrate your pendulum. Try these sample questions:

- Is my full name [name]?
- Was I born in the [city, state, country of birth]?
- Did I eat [type of food] for breakfast?

If you get accurate responses, keep going. You might also ask:

- Is it in my optimal interest to proceed with my questions using my pendulum right now? *If you get a no, make a plan to come back at a future time.*
- Is it best for me to revisit my questions at a future time? *If you get a yes, you can get specific and ask if you should work with your pendulum again in an hour, a day, a week, etc. Use your intuition to guide you.*

If the answers to basic questions leave you questioning the accuracy, it may be a good idea to regroup. Take a walk, meditate, or drink some tea or a fresh glass of water—whatever you like to do to decompress. Try again when you're ready.

Setting Intentions and Getting Grounded

Making the most of your pendulum relies on how it works with your energy for your optimal good. So much of how your pendulum works with your energy depends on how you frame your intentions and questions. Everything in this world carries positive and negative energy. Some refer to this as active and passive energy. Others think of this as heavy and light energy. Ultimately, we are talking about forces that interact to form a dynamic system in which the whole is greater than the assembled parts. It doesn't matter how you refer to this idea; whatever resonates with you is what's important. Never use a pendulum with the wrong intentions. When we coach our clients, we advise that they use their pendulums only for the highest good. By setting the right intentions, the guidance that you will receive from your intuition will be aligned with your highest good. If you can clarify what you want to know and set your intentions, it will be much easier to ask the right questions to unearth your answers.

Intention Setting

Setting an intention before your pendulum session is a powerful way to clarify and focus on what you are trying to achieve in the present moment. It creates meaning and purpose for your desires and aligns your mind and heart. Crafting powerful intentions starts by setting goals that align with your life's values, aspirations, and purpose. You'll want to make intention setting a regular part of your pendulum practice. Here's a brief guide on how:

- Try to write your intentions down. There is power in the physical act of writing.
- State your intention in a positive way. Instead of "I don't want to have low energy today," say, "I feel refreshed and energized today."
- Restate your intention out loud.
- Surrender your intention to the universe. This is very important. It may not always be easy, but it is necessary. Embrace the freedom of knowing that the universe has your back and you're not in control.
- Stay open and curious. There are infinite possibilities out there for each of us in every decision we make. The unknown is a very exhilarating place to live in. Getting comfortable with the uncomfortable and detaching from the outcomes is key.

Feel free to use your intention as a daily mantra that you repeat throughout the day, the week, or whatever length of time feels good to you. After your intentions are set, decide how you'd like to be guided on your pendulum journey. Determine whether you want to tap into your subconscious mind or get guidance from your higher self—the part of you that is connected to universal intelligence and has access to information beyond what your conscious mind is able to process.

Now let's begin!

Grounding Your Energy

You may already have gotten comfortable with using your pendulum, but here's a refresher and more guidance on getting grounded and doing deeper work.

Finding a place to still your mind and get grounded works best when seeking clarity about major decisions in life. We are all human and experience a multitude of emotions at any given time depending on our circumstances and external environment. If you go into your session in a neutral state and stay as open-minded as possible to the answers that you receive, you're more likely to get accurate results. In order to do this, it's best to be relaxed and comfortable.

Here's a grounding exercise to help you get started:

1. Find a comfortable place to get quiet and still your mind. There are many techniques to ground yourself, and please feel free to find what works best for you. We like to use breath work and visualization to move into a space of stillness.

2. Close your eyes and take four deep breaths. Inhale through your nose and count to four on the breath in; count to four as you exhale through your mouth with an audible sigh. Visualize tree roots growing from the soles of your feet. See them being planted deep underground into the core of the earth.

3. Envision a white light emanating from your heart and expanding outward to surround your body. You can think of this light as a cocoon of protection and a way to share your light. Sit with this vision and breathe deeply. You'll know when you're grounded when you feel present in your body. This can feel freeing, calming, and as if you're connected with the earth, the universe, or yourself. You may feel one of these ways, all of them, or something totally different. Trust that you'll know when you feel grounded and ready. Open your eyes and get started.

Diving In

After grounding and calibrating your pendulum, go ahead and begin exploring your inner world. You may know exactly what questions you have, and that is wonderful. Know that your answers may not always reflect what you think you want. That's okay. The reason you're getting a certain answer may not be apparent to you in the moment, but it's usually for your highest good. Your higher self, the part of you that is always connected to the universe, knows what is best for you.

As an example, let's pretend that you asked your pendulum about whether it is optimal for you to attend an event with friends at a restaurant on a certain date and got a no. After receiving this information, you decide to trust what your intuition is telling you and do not go. However, you feel a little FOMO (fear of missing out) and question whether you made the right decision. This is perfectly normal, but continue to believe in your decision. Fast forward to after the event. What happened while you weren't there? Maybe you got to catch up with your family and make amends with a loved one, or you were able to complete a work or school assignment during that time. Maybe everyone at the restaurant got food poisoning and the universe was trying to protect you from getting sick. We don't always know why we are receiving the answers that we get. However, as this scenario exemplifies, learning to trust your intuition won't steer you in the wrong direction. As you have more experiences like the made-up scenario above, you'll gain more confidence in your decisions and in yourself. Pretty soon, you'll stop questioning yourself altogether.

Know when to ask broad questions and when to get specific. If you know exactly what information you're seeking, try to be as specific as possible. For example, if you're wanting to know if you're in the right relationship, you might ask your pendulum the following question: "Is it for my most optimal good to be in a romantic relationship with Joe at this time?" State your questions with confidence and remember to use close-ended yes or no questions only.

If you're not certain how to frame a question for the most accurate response, a good place to start is with a broad question. In the following sample scenario, let's pretend that you're struggling with your job and contemplating whether to leave. Your session might go something like this: "Am I happy in my current career?" This is a broad question that can go in various directions and be interpreted in many different ways. If you get a yes, your intuition, at that moment in time, is guiding you toward staying in your current career path. If your pendulum shows you a no, keep exploring what that means for you. Perhaps you are to stay in your current industry, but it's time to find a new job. Perhaps it's time to explore a new industry altogether or start your own business.

Your next question might be this: "Is it in my optimal interest to stay in my current industry/profession?" If yes, you might go on to ask, "Is it in my best interest to look for a new job in the same industry?" If yes, start asking yourself what you've always dreamed of doing. As an example, if you've always wanted to be a writer, you may ask if it's in your best interest to begin writing a blog or submitting short stories to a magazine to try to get published. Perhaps you want to be a copywriter for an advertising agency. Ask, "Would it be beneficial for me to seek out a mentor/recruiter to help me determine the best path forward?" If anyone comes to mind, ask if they are the right person to connect with to help you.

If you don't know what you'd like to do next in your career, first brainstorm and write down any and all ideas. Ask a trusted friend to help you with this process if you're called to.

This is only one scenario of how your pendulum session could go. The process of exploring your heart's desires is exhilarating. It can also be scary, as the unknown can cause fear and anxiety for some. We encourage you to stay open to the infinite possibilities. If you're not ready to receive information, you don't have to ask. And if it's not in your best interest to receive a particular answer, your pendulum will communicate that by showing you a not now movement. All you have to do is trust.

Chapter 5
DIVINATION AND YOUR CONNECTION TO THE UNIVERSE

There are many forms of divination—reading tarot and oracle cards, interpreting tea leaves, casting runes, mediumship, scrying, and more. If you're reading this book and using a pendulum, you're probably curious about divination in some shape or form. Divination is an ancient practice that helps us connect to the spiritual realm and discover that which is hidden using our own energy and supernatural means. The practice of divination guides us to explore the deepest parts of ourselves and discover what lies beneath the surface. In this section, we'll explore a few ways to utilize your pendulum for divination. More specifically, we're going to take a look at how to use your pendulum to connect with your higher self; how to work with your angels and spirit guides; how to explore soul groups and past lifetimes; and how to use tarot and oracle decks, runes, and numerology. One thing to remember is that the pendulum is a tool. It alone does not hold the answers. You are the key. You and your higher self hold the knowledge to all the guidance you seek.

Meet Your Higher Self

Let's begin with your higher self. Your higher self is the all-knowing part of your soul that connects up to the universe, however you define the "universe." As mentioned before, whether you resonate with God, the Divine, the universe, Source, or any other term denoting a higher power, the underlying thread is that you believe in something bigger than yourself that is nonmaterial. Perhaps a simpler way to think about this is your soul or spirit. When you work with your pendulum, you are seeking to receive answers from your higher self.

Your higher self is much more than your physical body. It is the eternal soul consciousness that knows no limits. Answers from your higher self come from your heart, not your head. Many religions and ancient traditions teach us that when we connect with the universal consciousness, which we are all part of, we are connected to our higher selves. Your higher self is the part of you that is removed from your ego, which tends to keep you living in fear. Connecting with your higher self requires nothing outside of yourself. You're innately connected to your higher self, who knows what your purpose in life is and holds all the answers for you.

The Purpose of Your Ego

Just as we all have intuition, as humans, we also have an ego. Ego is the more critical and chaotic part of ourselves. The ego communicates through our five basic senses. The ego's only concern is itself; it can never have enough, and second place is not an option. Living from your ego is the opposite of living from your higher self through intuitive guidance. Don't worry, everyone has an ego. Part of functioning in society and operating in the modern world requires us to have one. We are really good at hearing and listening to our ego, which will communicate the loudest if you let it.

Our egos are prone to listening to societal conditioning. Often, we are exposed to unrealistic standards about beauty, material possessions, money, and relationships. These unhealthy expectations may lead us to feel insecure and anxious. When we tune in to our egos, we may become overly analytical and critical about ourselves and our present situation. This unhealthy behavior will create feelings of inferiority and lack of self-worth.

Despite these harmful influences, the ego does play an important role in your life. As you grow, the ego supports you in establishing and organizing your life through education, career, and starting a family. But watch out—the ego loves to seduce you into the illusion that you have control of your life and those around you. Many of us have begun to realize that there is more to life than materialism. Our spiritual journey shifts us from the constraints of our ego into the freedoms of our intuition. Your pendulum can help you bypass the constraints of your ego and open up the path to learning from a new perspective. Only from this deeper point of view can we truly exercise our free will.

For example, if you believe that the only way to earn a living is through a nine-to-five job at a large company, you will never entertain other ideas of earning a living for yourself. Opening your heart and mind to the opportunities you've never encountered before feeds the database of all the subconscious knowledge we store. As we begin to open up to new possibilities, a pendulum can be a helpful companion in practicing discernment. If you're not sure about a choice because it is outside of your previous limiting beliefs imposed by societal programming and ego, then tap in with your pendulum and explore the possibilities. When we trust that our higher self has the guidance we seek, we maximize the amount of free will we can access to create optimal outcomes for self and for all.

In our experience, we've found that most of us have not been raised to connect with our intuition and trust it. In fact, quite the opposite. Until you are able to develop and trust your intuition, your ego will continue to try to dominate. However, true fulfillment is not found when your ego is the primary voice in your life. Allowing your highest self to guide the experiences in your life is what leads to love and internal peace. This is what we're here to learn to do, with the pendulum being a fabulous tool to accompany you on your spiritual journey by helping you make the optimal choices for you.

Importance of Paying Attention to the Wisdom of Your Higher Self

If you're ready to set your ego aside for a moment and connect to the wisdom of your higher self with a pendulum, you'll connect to unlimited possibilities. Your higher self is the part of you that has access to your Akashic Record, which contains your life's blueprint. The Akashic Records are a sort of infinite library that stores everything about each soul—from your previous lifetimes to your present life and future. That's why it is vital to have a strong connection with your higher self. When you live in alignment with the inner wisdom and guidance available to you from your higher self, you become the best, most authentic version of yourself. Those moments of deep intuition and creative inspiration will become a bigger part of your life if you allow this communication to expand. Your higher self can assist you in accessing the information already available to you in your Akashic Records and embracing all your unique gifts and talents.

So how do you connect with your higher self? First, get to know your higher self by going inward. The ability to "tune in" and hear what your higher self is trying to tell you requires the time and space to get still. Find a way that works for you to remove any distractions and go within.

This next exercise will help you quiet your mind and gain access to your higher self. It is designed to let go of all the things that create busy chatter inside our minds and prevent us from being still. When we learn to quiet our minds and get still, we are ready to receive all the wisdom, inspiration, motivation, and many other benefits that our higher self wants us to have.

Exercise
QUIET YOUR MIND AND GET PRESENT

We use this exercise with our coaching clients and recommend you give it a try. It's quick and easy. This is a great practice to use *before* working with your pendulum or anytime you need to get focused and present.

Draw a box in a journal or on a piece of paper. We recommend using a separate journal dedicated to your pendulum practice to capture any visions and thoughts you get. In the box, write down anything that you need to let go of for the next twenty minutes (or however long you plan to work with your pendulum, sit in meditation, or recharge your personal battery). It can be anything that you're thinking about: what to make for dinner, work emails that are waiting to be answered, what you're going to wear on your date later that evening… By mentally removing the chatter in your head and placing it elsewhere, even for a defined period of time, you are creating an intentional time and space to get still.

If you don't have paper and a pen handy, try doing this exercise in your mind. Visualize a box or another container and think of anything and everything that needs to be set aside so that you have the energetic and mental space to get clear and present. Now imagine placing all those tasks in this container and shutting the lid.

Now you're ready to pay attention. Your higher self will communicate through whispers, images, and other means, often in between your thoughts. Learning the language of your higher self requires the ability to tune in to your clairs, which we discussed in chapter 1. The clairs are the ways in which you receive information for guidance. We all have the ability to listen to and interpret our inner guidance using various or all clairs in different ways.

Exercise
MEET YOUR HIGHER SELF

The pendulum is the perfect tool to help you connect with your intuition and make it the dominant voice you hear. Before you begin a pendulum session, we recommend that you say a prayer and ask that your higher self be present with you as you seek the answers that are for your highest, most optimal good. If the higher self is a new concept for you, you may want to start by simply asking a few questions. Think of your higher self as your lifelong best friend and mentor who has all the answers for you. What would you ask a friend whom you want to get to know better?

- "What is your name?" With this question, use your pendulum and refer to the alphabet chart in the appendix (see page 135) to spell out the name. Don't be alarmed if the name doesn't make sense or is unusually long. This is very normal in the spirit world.
- "Is it in my best interest to ask what my purpose in life is at this time?"
- "Would it help me to explore my ancestry through past-life regression?"

And so on. The way you get to know your higher self is highly personal, and as such, create a practice that feels right for you. Learn to pay attention and trust the answers you receive. The more you do this, the more your lurking ego will back away and begin to fade.

Spirit Guides, Angels, Archangels, and Soul Groups

It is said that we are all born into this world with at least one spirit guide—a being that is dedicated to us and has been with us in all our lifetimes. Our guide is always present and watching over us for our most optimal good. We are also surrounded by angels constantly. We believe this to be very true!

Spirit guides and angels have their own identities and personalities, much like other entities, including archangels, spirit animals, dragons, fairies, sprites, and more. This topic may be a whole new world for you. We are just scratching the surface in this book. However, if you'd like to learn more about spirit guides and otherworldly beings, check out our recommended authors and experts on the subject in the recommended resources section at the end of the book.

Spirit Guides

A soul that has reached a level of awareness and a point advanced enough to assist another soul to do the same is what we refer to as a spirit guide. Guides have incarnated as humans countless times and thus understand the human experience. Their ability to not judge, to hold compassion, and to embody love is at such a heightened level that, for most of us, it is inconceivable. From the time your soul was born, you most likely have had the same spirit guide through all your incarnations and lifetimes. Some of us have more than one primary guide. Our guides can take various forms, including deceased loved ones, elders, angels, archangels, spirit animals, and ascended masters. You can request guides at different points in your life to help you with a specific issue because you have free will.

Spirit guides have signed up to take on the role of being your guide. They did so deliberately and intentionally. It's important to know that they truly want to assist you. It's their job and what gives them meaning and purpose! However, they can't help you unless you ask. We encourage you to establish a relationship with your guides. One of our favorite authors on the subject, Jean Slatter, provides a great way to do this. In her book, *Hiring the Heavens*, she explains how to hire your spiritual team for just about anything you're needing help with. Per Slatter, your divine team of angels and guides is always there to guide you on your path. The more you ask for help, the easier it becomes to see and hear their guidance through your own intuitive downloads or signs from the universe.[33]

It is believed that you can have an endless amount of spirit guides. Guides are like friends who provide unconditional love and know more than what our conscious minds can grasp. They come into our lives at different times for varying purposes. Typically, we all have at least one personal spirit guide, but usually there are many. When you're called and ready to meet your spirit guides, you may begin to have visions and dreams that indicate their presence. They may send you nudges, whispers, signs, synchronicities, and musical messages. You may start to notice certain people or opportunities showing up on your path more frequently. It's very exciting! Call on them and connect with them. They are always with you, waiting to assist you. You can connect with them through quieting your mind and meditation.

Use your pendulum to learn names, how many spirit guides you have, and how to best communicate with them. There's no limit to what you can learn. Your spirit guides are there, working on your behalf behind the scenes, whether you sense them or not. Sometimes it's during the most challenging times in our lives that we can feel disconnected from the universe, yet this is when our spirit guides can and want to help us more than ever.

Angels

Different spiritual traditions describe the angelic realms in various ways. There seems to be agreement that there is a hierarchy of angels, and these groupings are organized by function—such as guardian angels, for example. Like spirit guides, angels are also available for direction and protection, and they embody unconditional love, compassion, and wisdom. According to Melanie Beckler at Ask-Angels.com, there are nine angel ranks (plus humans).[34]

According to Kyle Gray, a foremost expert on angels, author, speaker, and one of our favorite go-tos for angel guidance, angels are our constant companions, and have been with us since the day we were born.[35] As human begins,

---

33   Jean Slatter, *Hiring the Heavens: A Practical Guide to Developing Working Relationships with the Spirits of Creation* (Novato, CA: New World Library, 2005).

34   Melanie Beckler, "Angelic Hierarchy—Understanding the 9 Angel Ranks," Ask Angels, accessed September 25, 2023, https://www.ask-angels.com/spiritual-guidance/angelic-hierarchy/.

35   Kyle Gray, *Angel Prayers: Harnessing the Help of Heaven to Create Miracles* (London: Hay House UK, 2018), 11.

we operate under a spiritual law known as "free will." Angels work under this law too. What this means is that you have to invite them in to help you. Angels offer us so much love and support, but we have to acknowledge them and ask for help. Our favorite Kyle Gray quote from his *Angel Prayers* book is "Angels of light, thank you for illuminating the path to my spiritual growth. Increasing my connection and faith is my focus"[36] Gray also explains that when we are feeling burdened, angels can direct us to a place of safety.[37] But what about all the other days when we don't necessarily need a miracle? Those are also times when we have access to their love and guidance, and they want to hear from us. So give thanks to your angel team every day, not only when you're in crisis. Your pendulum is a great tool you can use to connect with your spiritual team.

Archangels

Archangels are supernatural beings in the higher realm of angels. They are known to be messengers from the universe who deliver messages and guidance when we are open to receiving it. We may call on specific archangels when we need a solution, guidance, or support. They play different roles and govern different areas of life. They are always available to help us out. All we have to do is ask. Some of the most well-known archangels are Michael, Raphael, Gabriel, and Uriel. For example, Archangel Michael is most often called for protection and Archangel Gabriel is called for clarity and guidance.

Archangels are sent by the universe to accomplish large tasks. For example, Archangel Gabriel is known for delivering important messages throughout history. If you're wondering which archangel you'd like to work with at this moment, check out the archangel chart on page 73.

We may call on specific archangels when we need a solution, guidance, or support. Archangels do not get tired and can be in more than one place at a time. They like it when we call them for help because in asking, we honor them by our belief that their presence can bring miracles into our lives. Here's the type of guidance or assistance archangels can provide:

---

36   Gray, *Angel Prayers*, 258.

37   Gray, *Angel Prayers*, 13.

Archangel Michael: A powerful protector who helps with releasing fear and worry.

Archangel Raphael: Helps with healing physical and mental ailments.

Archangel Gabriel: Messenger of new beginnings, communication, and strength.

Archangel Jophiel: Guides you to the state of love and seeing beauty within and around you.

Archangel Uriel: Helps you hear divine messages and feel the divine presence.

Archangel Azrael: Helps those ready to transition from physical life to the spirit world.

Archangel Chamuel: Helps with peace, compassion, and restoring order out of chaos.

Archangel Haniel: Helps us recognize our beauty within and connects us to our intuitive wisdom.

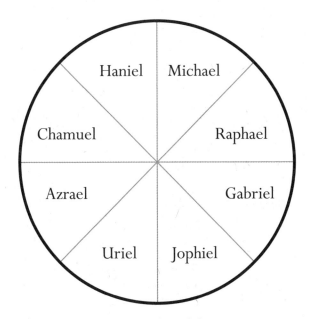

Figure 8: Archangel chart

If you'd like to work with other archangels, try drawing your own simple chart. These are a few other archangels to consider:

Archangel Ariel: Helps with happiness, abundance, and nature. Also helps those whose mission is aligned with assisting animals and nature.

Archangel Zadkiel: Helps with uplifting your vibration, love, forgiveness, mercy, and freedom.

Archangel Raziel: Helps you unearth the secrets and mysteries of the universe, develop your psychic abilities, and increase creativity.

Archangel Sandalphon: Works closely with musicians and others to assist with poetry and prayer.

Working with your higher self, spirit guides, angels, archangels, and other beings of light is a magical experience. By inviting them to be part of your pendulum session, you are honoring their presence and inviting their wisdom. Always remember to thank them for their work, guidance, unconditional love, and support. They love to be acknowledged by you.

Soul Groups

In the spirit world, across the veil, we all have soul families that we belong to in which we work together with other souls to accomplish various missions. These groups help us develop individually as well as collectively. All the work that we do in each of our lifetimes assists our primary soul family groups, our interlocking groups, and ultimately all other soul groups that are part of the universal consciousness. Our primary soul group consists of those souls who we incarnate with together in every lifetime. Think of this group as your first ring. Our interlocking soul groups include those souls who we incarnate and live multiple lifetimes with, but not in every lifetime. We may be part of a secondary group for very specific missions. This is your second ring group.

Each experience we go through is imperative to the overall evolution of the whole. Our personal experiences, lessons, and emotions are contributing to the overall knowledge of collective consciousness. Are you curious about who is in your soul family group or your interlocking soul group? You can access this information through working with your pendulum.

Exercise
DISCOVER YOUR SOUL FAMILY

Prepare for your pendulum session by getting grounded, setting your intention to discover who is in your soul family group, and connecting with your higher self. Calibrate your pendulum and think about your close family, your friends, and acquaintances. Think of someone who you feel very connected to. Ask your pendulum if they are in your soul family group. Wait for the yes or no answer and write down the results. If you get a no answer, you may ask if they are in your interlocking soul group. Keep track of your answers by documenting them in your journal, and pretty soon you'll have a very good idea who of your family, friends, and acquaintances are actually part of your soul group or interlocking soul group. This can help you understand family histories, challenges, and who you are here to work through life lessons with.

MARI'S STORY

I see 1104 everywhere—on receipts, mile markers, the digital clock on the oven, and the timestamp on a text message, to name a few places. Some days I see the number 1104 half a dozen times. My family and I assumed it was coincidental. It never occurred to me that someone could be sending me a sign as a way to make a connection. By working with my pendulum, gifted to me by Lana and Karina, I was able to ask questions and finally learn the significance of 1104.

A week later a butterfly floated by me while I was on a boat, in the middle of a lake, an odd sight to see a half mile from land. My pendulum helped me interpret this experience too. I'm happy to report that not only do I see butterflies and 1104 everywhere, but I know who is making the connection and adore receiving their love and support.

Numerology and Angel Numbers

Important numbers in our lives, such as our birthday, can help guide our most optimal path in life. This is an art form that is rooted in intuition. Numbers generate patterns that can help us tune in to the language of the universe. This language is used by our angels and guides to communicate with us on a daily basis.

When we formed HeartCentric Divine Creations, we began linking angel numbers to the pendulums that we create. This guidance showed up in a dream for Lana. Noticing angel numbers and interpreting the messages they hold at the moment they show up is another way to connect to the wisdom of the universe and to yourself. Numbers carry specific vibrational meaning. We encourage you to spend time creating a bond with your pendulum, explore angel numbers with your pendulum, and find the divine within.

Numerology

Numerology is the study of relationships between numbers, letters, and patterns in a mystical way. Every number has its own vibration and meaning in numerology. Numerology is a fascinating discipline that dates back thousands of years and has an energetic influence on our lives. Numbers are symbols that carry energetic vibrations that impact people on a celestial level. It is yet another practice that provides insights into your inner wisdom and helps you connect to your intuition. Like other methods of divination, numerology is a tool that is used to gain a deeper knowledge of the self, others, and how we relate to the world. Your numerology chart contains key insights that can be used to reveal your life purpose as well as give your insights about future possibilities.

There are many scholars, scientists, and religious leaders who believe that numbers are the essence of everything. Pythagoras, the founder of geometry, who also founded a school in Crotone, Italy, taught his students that each number had its own particular vibration and set of unique characteristics. This led him to divide the human soul into nine different variations. The numbers 1 through 9 are still used today in numerology, to which all other numbers, except for master numbers (11, 22, 33) are reduced. Zero is not used in numerology. For example, the number 10 would be reduced to 1 (1 + 0 = 1). The number 45 would be reduced to 9 (4 + 5 = 9).[38]

While the deep-rooted history of numerology and all that it encompasses is a topic too vast to cover in this book, we will touch on how numerology relates to angel numbers and how your pendulum can help you gain a deeper understanding of yourself.

---

38   Michael Johnstone, *The Book of Divination* (London: Sirius, 2022), 152–61.

Arguably the most important number of the main numbers in numerology is your life path number, which unearths your destiny in terms of the person you are meant to be and what challenges you may need to experience in order to learn and grow into that person. "Understanding the meaning of your Life Path number helps you see why things happen the way they do and gives you the power to move through any situation with purpose and intention," shares Numerology.com. "Your Life Path number is not only the most important of the core numbers, it's the most significant number in your whole Numerology chart."[39] You can find your life path number by reducing your birthday until you get to a single digit. For example, if your birthday is October 11, 1985, your life path number is 8. Let's break down the process of calculating:

10 (month) + 11 (day of month) + 1985 (year)
Month reduced: $1 + 0 = \mathbf{1}$
Day reduced: $1 + 1 = \mathbf{2}$
$1985 = 1 + 9 + 8 + 5 = 23, 2 + 3 = \mathbf{5}$
$1 + 2 + 5 = \mathbf{8}$

If your life path number is 11, 22, or 33, you do not reduce it further. These are considered master numbers and represent an amplified variation on their root numbers. Master numbers imply tremendous potential for success juxtaposed by greater challenges and have their own meanings and interpretations. There are many resources and books available if you'd like to learn more numerology and your specific life path number. We recommend the book *Numerology for Beginners* by Gerie Bauer.

Vibrational frequencies of each life path number are unique and impact us in different ways. Since working with a pendulum requires you to tap into your vibrational frequencies as well as those surrounding you, angel numbers and numerology are staples of our daily practice.

---

39   "Master Numbers Hold the Powerful Potential in Numerology," Numerology.com, accessed September 25, 2023, https://www.numerology.com/articles/your-numerology-chart/core-numbers-numerology/.

Angel Numbers

Do you ever look at the clock and see 11:11 regularly? Have you noticed you're seeing 444 often or other repeating numbers in general? Do you wonder what they mean? Angel numbers are repeating sequences of numbers that may show up just about anywhere. It's easy to cast these sequential numbers aside and chalk them up to coincidence. However, they hold significant and powerful messages for you, so it's important to pay attention when you see them. Angel numbers are closely "connected to numerology" and considered an "offshoot."[40] Some believe that angel numbers, just like numerology, stemmed from Pythagoras—the Greek philosopher and founder of many mathematical and scientific discoveries, including the Pythagorean theorem. That means people have been taking note of these numbers and their deeper significance since the sixth century BC! Numbers hold much significance in our everyday lives, and because they are everywhere, our angels and guides use them to communicate with us.

You can harness the power of angel numbers and your pendulum and apply it to your everyday life. One easy way to do this is to pay attention to the angel numbers you're seeing. When a repeating number shows up for you, take a moment to pause, interpret the message, and reflect, as these are messages from the spiritual realm. Pay attention to the messages associated with the angel numbers that are showing up for you. When you want to go deeper to interpret the message your angels are sending you, this is a perfect time to work with your pendulum. Start asking deeper questions about how this particular message is relevant to your life at this moment in time. Keep asking whether there's something particular you need to act on. If you get a no, ask if this is the right moment to surrender to the universe. Trust your inner wisdom and know that divine guidance is always available to you.

Basic Angel Numbers and Their Meanings

111 Angel Number: Answer the call of your soul and make changes that bring you closer to what you really need in order to make spiritual progress. Angel number 111 is all about manifestation. It asks you to

40   Hans Decoz, "The History and meaning of Angel Numbers," World Numerology, accessed September 25, 2023, https://www.worldnumerology.com/blog/angel-numbers.html.

focus your thoughts, feelings, and ideas on what you want and pay close attention to what comes up for you. Try to focus on the positive and release what does not serve you as your thoughts become your reality. When you see the number 111, know that you are creating the life that you desire, so ask for optimal outcomes!

222 Angel Number: Your divine guidance is to stop worrying. Everything is working out just as it is supposed to. Trust that you are on the right path. Good things do happen. Angel number 222 is a sign that you are on the right track and doing the right things in life. This number is also bringing you happiness, good fortune, and joy. Look on the bright side of things and be happy. You are at a point where you need a sense of peace, trust, and balance in your life. When you see angel number 222, this is no coincidence. It's a divine message from your angels asking you to pay attention to their message.

333 Angel Number: You are called to commit yourself to your personal and spiritual development. Use your gifts and talents to assist others. If you keep seeing the angel number 333, your life purpose is what the angels are asking you to pay attention to. Everyone comes into this world with their own set of unique gifts and talents. It's important to understand what these are for you so that you can use them for optimal outcomes for all—including yourself. We spend our lifetime understanding what our soul's mission is, whether it's apparent to us or not. The 333 angel number asks us to develop our individual purpose and recognize that we're ready to do so. The universe always has our back, so trust the process and don't let fear stand in your way.

444 Angel Number: Your guardian angels are near and ready to help you. All you have to do is call on them. The 444 angel number is confirming that you are on the right path, whether it's apparent to you or not. If you're feeling defeated and ready to give up, this angel number is presenting itself to encourage you not to give up. When you see 444, your angels are as close as they can get, rooting for you and helping you achieve what you've set out to do. They are asking you to trust that everything is happening as it should and to call on them when you need a pick-me-up. Angel number 444 invites you to recognize the value of persistence, so don't give up and know that you will get to your destination on divine timing.

555 Angel Number: You are about to experience exciting, positive changes that will transform your life. Angel number 555 indicates that change is imminent. We all experience change in our lives. Sometimes change can seem intimidating or even scary, because we are stepping onto unfamiliar ground. When you see angel number 555, know that the change that is coming is for your highest good. Pay close attention to the guidance you are receiving from your angels, guides, and the universe and trust that the change you are experiencing is leading you toward a positive transformation.

666 Angel Number: While the number 666 has developed a bad reputation, from a spiritual perspective, this number signifies that your angels are encouraging you to reshift your focus. The number sequence 666 may show up to let you know that you are sacrificing too much of yourself from a mind, body, or soul perspective, and it's time to make some changes. If you can ease your grip around your situation and let go of your need for control, you allow for life to flow with more ease. It's time to shift your perspective!

777 Angel Number: Your plans are becoming reality. Stay positively focused and open to the messages that the universe is sending to you. The work that you put into your personal growth and development is paying off. You have come a long way, and angel number 777 is a reminder that you should keep going. Keep learning from your past experiences but also use them to guide you to manage your present and future. Your learnings in this lifetime are bringing you closer and closer to manifesting the dream life you are imagining.

888 Angel Number: It is time for you to start making a few changes in your life. Prepare yourself for the riches to come. When you see angel number 888, start paying close attention to the opportunities in your life that may lead you on a journey toward financial abundance. It is time to open up your heart and mind to possibilities. Share your gifts and talents with the universe, and the universe will reward you with gifts beyond your current comprehension.

999 Angel Number: This is a fresh beginning to take you to a higher, more enlightened path. It's time to take flight. You are always guided and supported by the universe. Your angels are helping bring closure to a chapter in your life so that you can begin a new chapter that will take you toward greater levels of love, joy, abundance, and freedom. Put your fears aside and step into this new chapter with courage. If you are needing more guidance from your divine team of guides and angels, all you have to do is ask. When you ask, you shall receive. Just pay attention because you never really know how the guidance will show up. Just trust that it will show up at the perfect moment.

1111 Angel Number: It is time to find your own truth and align it with your life, your thoughts, and your actions. Angel number 1111 is one of the luckiest, most powerful numbers. When you see this magical number over and over, it is the universe letting you know that you are on the right track. Ensure that your thoughts and actions are always aligned with your personal truth. When you live your life grounded in your truth, your spiritual team is working behind the scenes to propel you forward to living your most joyous life. This is your confirmation that you are well on your way. Keep moving forward and trust in the universe.

We learned more about angel numbers through spiritual teacher Kyle Gray's work, which was very inspiring to us. When angel numbers show up, we are blessed to receive guidance, information, or a blessing from the universe. We love this prayer from *Raise Your Vibration*: "Thank you, angels, for revealing to me what I need to know."[41]

Because angel numbers and numerology are two different aspects of the same system, they provide us with guidance and clarity when we tune in. While angel numbers hold a message for us at a particular moment in time, numerology gives us a deeper look within ourselves, our spiritual path, and what we are here to accomplish in this lifetime.

Try the fun exercise that follows to explore what angel numbers are most optimal to work with in conjunction with your pendulum.

---

41   Kyle Gray, *Raise Your Vibration: 111 Practices to Increase Your Spiritual Connection* (Carlsbad, CA: Hay House, 2016), 19.

Exercise
ANGEL NUMBERS AND YOUR PENDULUM

After getting grounded and setting your intentions, use the following chart to ask your pendulum which angel number you need to work with to receive the most optimal guidance for your situation or question.

- Hold your pendulum in the center of the wheel and state, "Please show me which number has the guidance I need at this time."
- Let the pendulum begin moving. It will swing toward a number in the wheel.
- If you're not sure which number it is pointing to specifically, ask it to confirm. For example, if you're in between the numbers 222 and 333, ask "Is 222 the number most optimal for me at this time?" If you get a no, ask if 333 is the correct number. You should receive your answer quickly.

The angel number descriptions can be referenced to help you understand the meanings of the messages you're getting. Trust what your intuition is telling you, and if you need further clarification, ask your pendulum more questions and ask whether or not you're interpreting the messages correctly.

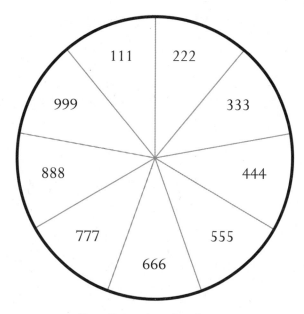

Figure 9: Angel number diagram

Forms of Divination

When searching for clarity and guidance, tarot cards, oracle cards, runes, numerology, and many other forms of divination, when used in combination with a pendulum, allow you to gain insights into your past, present, and future. These forms of divination help identify obstacles and challenges you may face and can help you navigate what direction to take. Taking action in a way that you (or your higher self) validates is empowering.

Tarot and Oracle Cards

Tarot is a form of divination that allows you to connect to your higher self and intuition and that can help lead you down your most optimal path and fulfill your karma. At a basic level, it is a system of cards depicting various characters and archetypes. Symbolically, tarot cards convey a journey that we as humans can relate to because we all travel our own unique paths from the time of birth. Traditional tarot decks consist of seventy-eight cards (the major and minor arcana) that are laid out in various spreads.

Tarot originated in Europe in the fifteenth century and has a rich history and following in many cultures. Tarot decks can range from simple to complex. While early tarot card decks were beautiful, hand-painted works of art, modern tarot decks come in as many styles as imaginable.

The main difference between tarot and oracle cards is that tarot has a predictable structure and rules, whereas oracle cards have no set number or structure. Tarot is typically interpreted with a standard structure and common definitions. Oracle decks contain any kind of content and can have as many cards as the creator chooses, typically between thirty-six and sixty-four. One way to think of tarot cards is that they are like pages in a book. Each card is one page of the story. Oracle cards are like the whole chapter and communicate a larger portion of the story. How you choose to shape your practice with tarot and oracle cards, as with any part of your spiritual journey, is completely up to you. Explore, practice, and have fun!

Using Your Pendulum with Tarot or Oracle Cards

If you are shopping for a tarot or oracle card deck, working with a pendulum is a fantastic way to help you decide which deck is optimal for you. Simply hold your pendulum over the deck that you're considering and ask if this is your optimal deck. If you get a no, go to another deck you're drawn to and ask again. Pretty soon you'll be the proud owner of a deck that is the right one for you at that time.

If you own several decks and are not sure which deck to work with at the moment, ask your pendulum to show you which deck is right for you at this time. Simply ask, "Is it in my most optimal interest to work with this deck at this time?"

Your pendulum can also be helpful in determining how many cards to pull if you're not sure. Just ask, "Is it ideal to pull one card today?" If you get a no, keep going until your pendulum shows you a yes.

If you are not sure which cards to pull, a pendulum may help. Spread your cards out in front of you. Ask the pendulum to show you a yes when you hover over the optimal card to pull. Hold your pendulum over your cards and move it slowly across them until you see it moving in the yes direction. That is your sign that you found the card to pull.

Another great way to use your pendulum is to confirm whether you're understanding the card's guidance. After pulling the card and interpreting the message, you may ask your pendulum a series of questions about the guidance that showed up. Just remember to trust the process and have faith in the guidance you're receiving. If the message is not clear at this moment, come back later that day or the next day for more clarity through your pendulum work. Clarity shows up in divine time.

Runes

Runes are another ancient form of oracle and method of connecting to one's higher self and inner guidance for divination. The most well-known runic alphabet, the Elder Futhark, holds twenty-four letters. Runes are an ancient practice shrouded in mystery. Since this ancient practice was developed before many people were literate, there are a wide variety of potential meanings attributed to runes.

"Using runes is a great way to tap into our intuition, access our inner voice and perform divination," write Talisa and Sam of *Two Wander*. "Traditionally, runes were cast in multiples of 3, or at the very least odd numbers. There are a few 5-rune layouts that are most commonly used, a couple of 7 and 9-rune layouts that are also often used, and a 24-rune layout that is usually done at the beginning of a year (whether that be your new birth year, winter solstice or actual New Year's Day), to forecast what the year ahead holds."[42] While there are many different types of rune layouts, you can start with a simple one-rune pull for a yes/no type answer or feel for the day.

You can experiment with adding pendulum work to your runes practice. One way to do so is to cast the runes on a surface and use your pendulum to select which runes to read and in what order. Like with tarot, ask your pendulum to confirm whether what you're interpreting is accurate. There are no limits to the ways that you can create your own cast if you use your imagination. Explore what works for you.

---

42 Talisa and Sam, "Rune Meanings and How to Use Rune Stones for Divination," *Two Wander* (blog), accessed September 25, 2023, https://www.twowander.com/blog /rune-meanings-how-to-use-runestones-for-divination.

Synchronicities and
Other Signs from the Universe

When you are in alignment with the universe, your guides, angels, and higher self will keep sending you messages and signs to let you know that you are on your path. Synchronicity, as defined by Carl Jung, is "a *meaningful coincidence* of two or more events where something other than the probability of chance is involved."[43] For example, have you ever gotten a call from a friend who happens to be a nurse just as you were about to pick up the phone and call her for advice about an ailing parent? Or perhaps you met the perfect videographer just as you were searching for someone to help you create videos for work. Consider these synchronicities and reinforcement that you are on an optimal path for healing and personal growth.

How do you know that what you're experiencing is truly synchronicity and not just pure coincidence? This is where your pendulum can help. Simply connect with your intuition and ask.

Signs from the universe show up in other ways besides angel numbers and synchronicities. Your sign may be an animal, a flower, a song, or even a dream. If you're not sure what your sign is, you can ask. According to Gabby Bernstein, number-one *New York Times* bestselling author, spiritual teacher, and motivational speaker, "You can ask for a sign to guide you toward anything you desire. If you're unsure about a decision or you simply want to know you're on the right track, ask for a sign. And don't get hung up about what your sign should be. Just choose the first thing that comes to your mind." Gabby also recommends, "Once you ask for your sign, the next step is crucial. You must turn over your desire to the universe with a prayer. Say this prayer: 'Thank you, Universe, for offering me clarity. Show me my sign if I'm moving in the right direction.' Then be patient."[44]

When you're in alignment with the universe and you receive your sign, it will be crystal clear. You won't miss it. Receive it as a gift and thank the universe for the reinforcement. Over time, you'll notice that your sign or signs

---

43   C. G. Jung, *The Collected Works of C. G. Jung: Complete Digital Edition*, vols. 1–19, ed. Gerhard Adler and R. F. C. Hull (Princeton, NJ: Princeton University Press, 2014), 520.

44   Gabby Bernstein, "How to Ask the Universe for a Sign," GabbyBernstein.com, accessed September 25, 2023, https://gabbybernstein.com/secret-asking-universe-sign-trusting-guidance-receive/.

will keep showing up over and over. Once this starts to happen regularly, pause in that moment, pay attention, and reflect. The universe may be sending you a message. What were you doing at that moment? What were you thinking about? When the message you just received isn't clear to you, that's a perfect time to pick up your pendulum and start asking questions.

Chapter 6
PRACTICAL APPLICATIONS

There are endless uses for your pendulum. It's a wonder why this tool isn't used more often. In this chapter, we are going to explore some practical pendulum applications that you can begin applying to your everyday life. As you go through your day, you are constantly faced with decisions to make, whether big or small. It may be as inconsequential as "Is it optimal to eat pancakes for breakfast today?" or a larger choice, such as "Is it in my best interest to move to New York City this year?" Whether you're a pro at confidently making decisions or tend to be indecisive, your AGA will assist you every day if you put it to use. In the appendix at the end of this book you'll find a Pendulum Session Planning Guidesheet that can be used to assist you in your preparation.

Let's explore a few key areas where you may find your pendulum to be helpful: energy healing, relationships, business and career, finances, prioritizing your day, finding missing objects, travel, and pets.

Clearing Energy

Energy is vibrating everywhere. It is around us, within us, and in a constant state of disseminating and receiving. Since you are an electromagnetic being, your experiences and relationships will attract frequencies that match your own. That's why it's important to be inside of and surrounded by the highest vibrations that your body can process. Sometimes, we're aware of positive energies around, such as happy vibes from someone who just landed their dream job. Often, we are equally sensitive to the negative energies bouncing off someone who's in a bad mood. We aren't always aware of it, but as energy accumulates around us, over time it becomes stagnant and can turn into negative energy. When exposed to negative energy, we start to feel down and out of balance, which can lead to emotional, mental, and physical consequences. Pendulums are an amazing tool that you can use to help clear and remove unwanted energies to bring you in alignment with your best, most joyful self.

Chakras: Your Spiritual Batteries

We are so much more than a physical body. We are energy. Inside your aura—the subtle energy body that surrounds and protects you—are seven energy centers called *chakras*. These centers relate to our emotional and spiritual systems and our overall well-being. One of our favorite ways to use our pendulums is to determine which chakras are out of balance or blocked and open them. Releasing blocks is important in helping us feel more balanced and in flow. You can do this too, for yourself and for others. In the next exercise, we will explain how. But first, let's explore what the chakras are and how they work.

Chakra translates to "wheel" from Sanskrit. There are seven major energy centers, or chakras, running down the center of your body from the base of your spine to the crown of your head. This vital life force allows our energy to flow through us freely. In Sanskrit, this energy is referred to as *prana*. Each wheel is constantly spinning and is associated with different types of health, expressions, and abilities.

You can think of your chakras as your spiritual batteries. When all your batteries are working optimally, you will feel more balanced and in flow with life. When your batteries contain too much charge or lack energy, they can become tired or out of balance, which can impact your emotional, mental, and physical health. For example, when your throat chakra is low in energy, you may have difficulty expressing your truth and other particular qualities associated with that chakra. Chakras are dynamic, and as such, we can expect to have imbalances—most likely on a daily basis. This is normal. As your body, mind, and spirit are interconnected, unbalanced chakras can affect one another. That is why it is important to check your chakras and keep them flowing regularly.

Your pendulum is a great tool to determine where your spiritual batteries are low in energy and recharge them. And when you do, you will feel lighter, more in sync with yourself, and better overall.

Figure 10: The seven chakras

Seven Main Chakras: The Basics

Root Chakra

The root chakra is located at the base of your spine and is represented by the color red. It represents our foundation and allows us to feel grounded and connected to the earth. The root chakra controls survival, financial security, stability, and overcoming challenges. It is associated with the earth element.

Sacral Chakra

The sacral chakra is located about two inches below the navel. It controls our pleasure, sexual energy, creativity, our sense of well-being, and abundance. It is associated with the water element and represented by the color orange.

Solar Plexus Chakra

The solar plexus chakra is located in the upper abdomen. It controls our confidence, self-worth, and self-esteem. It is associated with the fire element and the color yellow.

Heart Chakra

The heart chakra in the center of our chest, just above the heart. It represents our ability to give and receive love. It is associated with the air element and the color green.

Throat Chakra

The throat chakra is located in your throat and is represented by the color blue or turquoise. This chakra has to do with our ability to communicate authentically, how we express ourselves, influence others, and speak our truth. It is associated with the ether element.

Third Eye Chakra

The third eye chakra is located on our forehead, right between the eyes. It represents our ability to see beyond the current situation and connect to our intuitive wisdom. It is associated with the element of light and is colored indigo.

Crown Chakra

The crown chakra is located at the very top of our heads. It controls our connection to the Divine. It is associated with the element of Divine Consciousness and is violet in color.[45]

Exercise
BALANCING CHAKRAS TO CLEAR YOUR ENERGY

There are many complex approaches to chakra health. We use an easy and basic exercise for chakra balancing and healing with the help of the pendulum. You can use this exercise on yourself if you're feeling low vibrationally or imbalanced. To achieve the best results and the

---

45 "Chakra Basics," International Association of Reiki Professionals, accessed November 6, 2023, https://iarp.org/chakra-basics/.

highest vibrations, it's important to incorporate your intentions into the process of clearing and opening chakras.

How to Check for Imbalances or Blocks

1. Start by going through the initial process to prepare: Connect within and state your source from where you would like your answers to come. Get grounded and calibrate your pendulum to confirm your yes and no.

2. Now, check each chakra. Using the diagram on page 91, starting at the root (or base) chakra, hold the pendulum over the area and ask if that chakra is open. Simply say, "Is my [insert chakra] open?" If you don't have the diagram near, visualize the color associated with each spinning disc in your mind's eye while you ask if the chakra is open.

3. Your pendulum will show you a yes or no. If it stands still, this may mean it is completely blocked.

4. Work your way up to the crown chakra, asking if each of the seven chakras are open one by one.

5. Take note of which chakras you receive a no for. If you need to, have a pen and paper handy to write it down.

After you check all seven chakras, it is time to open the chakras that are imbalanced or blocked.

How to Open the Chakras

1. Now program your pendulum to show you what direction it swings to remove stagnant or unwanted energy. You can say, "Show me the motion to remove unwanted energy to open and clear my chakras." For most, this will be a counterclockwise circle, which indicates that the chakra is out of balance or restricted. If the pendulum does not move at all, this indicates that the chakra is blocked. However, your movement may be different, so it's important to ask your pendulum to show you.

2. Now ask the pendulum to show you what locking in positive energy looks like for you. Typically, this will be a clockwise motion. Again, ask your pendulum what the motion is for you.

3. Remember your movement for clearing? If you don't, ask your pendulum to show you the movement to clear again. Then hold the pendulum over the imbalanced chakra and ask to clear it.

4. Let the pendulum begin to spin on its own. Visualize that undesired energy leaving your body from the source of where you're feeling it as you let the pendulum swing. Watch it move in the clearing direction until it stops. For both of us authors, the movement to remove stagnant energy or blocks is a counterclockwise circle. This is the case for most people we know, but please do test your movement when you are first getting acquainted with your pendulum.

5. Let the pendulum swing and clear the chakra until it stops on its own. Now make a swishing motion to move any negative, stagnant, imbalanced energy out. You can visualize it leaving or moving out of a window. Say thank you and go to the next blocked chakra to perform the same ritual.

6. After you finish opening each restricted or blocked chakra, you'll want to ask if all the chakras have been opened. For example, you can say, "Is my root chakra now open? Is my heart chakra now open?" Ask about each chakra that you cleared and opened. If you get a yes to each one, you're all set. If you get a no, go back and clear the chakra that still needs work.

Locking in Clear and Positive Energy

When all of your chakras are opened, you'll want to lock in the positive energy.

1. Hold the pendulum over each cleared chakra and say, "Please lock in the loving and positive energy for my highest good and the highest good of all." Use your own words as you see fit to bring in positive energy.

2. Let the pendulum swing in the direction of locking in clear, positive energy until it stops on its own. Typically this will be a clockwise motion, which indicates that the energy is moving freely and is balanced. As before, please test your movement when you are first getting acquainted with your pendulum.

3. Say thank you and go to the next chakra that was opened to perform the same ritual.

4. Close out by giving gratitude to the source that resonates with you—your higher self, the universe, spirit guides, angels, ascended masters, and so on.

There are many benefits to opening the chakras, the largest being that your energy can flow freely through the mind and body. Following this chakra-clearing exercise and over the next couple of days after, you should feel lighter, connected, more positive energy, and balanced. Removing what does not serve you gives you a sense of calm and focused intention in your body, not only physically but emotionally and spiritually as well. Stay hydrated and nourished to continue to feel the benefits.

Exercise
BALANCING AND OPENING CHAKRAS FOR OTHERS

Once you've mastered clearing your own chakras, you may be ready to take the energy-clearing exercise a step further and help others do the same. You can use your pendulum to do this, assuming you have their permission. Follow the same steps as for solo chakra work, but adjust the exercise as follows:

1. Begin by going through the initial process to prepare. Doing this together can be a powerful way to connect with one another.

2. Have your friend lie down and ask them to connect to their body. Have them try to pinpoint where they're feeling the unwanted energy.

3. Hover your pendulum over each chakra over their body, working your way up from the root to the crown. For each chakra, ask "Is [your friend's name]'s root chakra open?" Your pendulum will give you a yes or no or stand still over those that need attention.

4. Next, follow the steps for how to open the chakras (page 93) and locking in positive energy (page 94).

5. When all the chakras are opened and you've brought in the positive energy, remember to close out by giving gratitude to the source that resonates with you or with them.

This exercise can be done for someone else virtually if you have their permission. The balancing chakras exercise requires focus and heartfelt attunement to yourself and to the other person you're helping. Know that you are helping them heal with the assistance of your pendulum. How awesome is that?

Auras: Energetic Fields of Protection

The aura is an invisible energy force that encompasses all living things at all times. Keeping your aura healthy and intact contributes to your body's overall well-being. A damaged aura can be detected with the use of a pendulum. Your aura extends beyond your physical body. It is a magnetic field that picks up on the emotions of others and on circumstances around you. When we are in stressful situations, it is possible to weaken or create tears in our auric field. As a result, we become more irritable, depressed, tired, and energetically depleted. We may even experience illness as a result of a weakened immune system. If you are experiencing a recurring strong emotion such as anger or anxiety, that may be an indication that you're keeping yourself stuck in that emotion, which could be a result of a tear in the auric field.

There are people who can see other people's auras and quickly identify where the auric damage is. If you can't see auras, you can still find the location by scanning the body with a pendulum. If you are scanning your own auric field, you can use a drawing of an outline of a body. Your aura is a bubble that extends above you, beneath you, in front of you, behind you, and to either side, up to three feet, so the damaged portion may be close or further away from the body. After you have identified the part of the aura that needs repairs, you can use a pendulum technique similar to opening chakras to repair the tears.[46]

Exercise
AURA REPAIR

Program your pendulum to show you what direction it moves to repair the tears in your auric field. You can say, "Show me my motion to repair the tears in my auric field." Then hold the pendulum over the damaged area and ask the pendulum to repair it. Allow the pendulum to begin spinning on its own. Visualize the auric field repairing while you let the pendulum swing. Use your imagination and know that whatever image or feeling comes through is right for you. Let it go until it stops. When finished, hold the pendulum over the repaired area and say, "Please lock in the loving and positive energy for my highest good and the highest good of all." Remember to give gratitude when you've completed the exercise. You can practice this technique on others or on yourself. We suggest implementing a regular practice of checking and balancing your chakras and your auric field for optimal health and wellness.

Clearing Energy in Spaces

Our homes and other areas we visit or spend time at can hang on to energy that isn't serving us. We can transform our spaces into safe havens infused with positive energy and create joyful, energetic environments that contribute to our overall well-being. If you just moved into a new home or have gone through a major transition, we highly recommend that you clear your space.

---

46   Maggie Percy and Nigel Percy, *Pendulums: For Guidance and Healing* (London: Flame Tree Publishing, 2021), 101–2.

Ideally, start out with cleaning out any clutter in your space before you focus on the energetic clearing. Here are some tips on how to clear and re-energize your surroundings:

1. Set your intention to cleanse the space from any energies that are not serving you. For example, you could set the intention to cleanse negative energy from your home so you can feel more creative. Another example is to set an intention to clear any negative energy that may prevent you from moving forward in your life in the most optimal way.

2. Open your window and smoke cleanse the space you are planning on clearing. As mentioned earlier, we recommend that you purchase a consciously sourced herb bundle. Try bundles that contain lavender, cedar, rosemary, mint, pine, or lemon balm, since these are sustainable sources. Burn your herb bundle in the space you're clearing while reciting your intention to cleanse the space of unwanted energies.

3. Get grounded by doing an easy grounding exercise from chapter 4. Then, calibrate your pendulum for yes and no.

4. Ask your pendulum to show you the movement for clearing energy. For us, it rotates in a counterclockwise circular motion. After establishing your energy clearing movement, allow the pendulum to begin swinging while you repeat your intention out loud or in your head. In your mind's eye, visualize the energy being released and transmuted into the ethers. You can picture a white light, a golden light, a pink light, or whatever image feels right for you—there is no right or wrong. Let the image of the unwanted energy clearing out of your space permeate your whole being and the space around you.

5. When finished clearing your space, your pendulum will slow down and come to a stop. Now visualize your space being infused with positive, renewed energy. However this shows up for you is absolutely perfect.

6. Next, ask your pendulum to lock in the positive energy that you are ushering in. Calibrate your pendulum to lock in positive energy. For example, if your pendulum moves in a counterclockwise circle to clear the energy, then you may get a clockwise circle motion for locking in

the energy. Whatever movement you get, take notice of it and feel good about all the positive energy that is being infused into your space. Let the pendulum move to lock in all that positivity until it slows down and comes to a stop.

7. Finally, give gratitude and thank your higher self, your spirit guides, and any other helpers who you resonate with for their assistance. This is important and it is recommended not to skip this rewarding step. Congratulations! You have just completed a beautiful ceremony to clear your space.

Quieting Our Minds for Overall Well-Being

In the age of technology, social media, and the acceleration of life as we know it, we get caught up in the day-to-day hustle that puts us on autopilot. With the media bombarding us with news designed to provoke fear and anxiety, this way of life can take a physical, emotional, and mental toll on our overall well-being. Using a pendulum can help us slow down, reflect, and deeply connect with ourselves. Pendulums are an excellent tool to work with to lower brain waves and turn down the mental noise. They can help us pause and recalibrate ourselves. In order to better understand how a pendulum can help your overall wellness by lowering your brain waves, let's dive deeper into the five different states of brain waves.

Five Brain Wave States

- Gamma is the highest state, associated with focus and insight, typically firing when the brain is concentrating and learning.
- Beta is the state that we mostly experience. It allows us to focus and is critical for reading, writing, and socializing.
- Alpha is the state that we shift into when we are relaxed, such as taking a bath or getting ready to go to bed.
- Theta is the meditative state also associated with that hypnotic flow that creates peak performance or autopilot mode of doing something we have done repetitively in the past, such as driving a car. When we are in a theta state, we are allowing insights and solutions to enter because our

minds are not processing the noisy chatter we've gotten accustomed to listening to all day every day.

- Delta is the state where we experience that deep, restorative, dreamless sleep.[47]

Let's further explore the theta state. Dr. Joe Dispenza beautifully summarizes the benefits of the theta state. His cutting-edge research in conjunction with the HeartMath Institute has found that training your brain to a new more coherent mind requires the unconscious mind, where your autonomic nervous system lives, to take over.[48] It can't be done by force or will with your conscious mind. The autonomic nervous system is your operating system that actually runs the show and controls all these patterns. So the deeper you get into theta brain waves, the slower your brain waves get, which allows your autonomic nervous system to take over.[49]

Physical healing happens when your body reaches a deep level of relaxation and you move out of the sympathetic nervous system state into the parasympathetic nervous system state. The theta state also helps release hormones that restore our immune systems. Additionally, the theta brain wave state activates your creativity, your brain's right hemisphere. This is when creative solutions to problems show up as well as new inspiration and ideas.

Theta Meditation

According to the National Center for Complementary and Integrative Health, "the term 'meditation' refers to a variety of practices that focus on mind and body integration and are used to calm the mind and enhance overall well-being. Some types of meditation involve maintaining mental focus on a particular sensation, such as breathing, a sound, a visual image, or a mantra, which is a repeated word or phrase. Other forms of meditation include the practice of mindfulness, which involves maintaining attention or awareness of the present

47   Erin Magner, "Brainwaves—For Better Health, Sleep, and Focus," Well and Good, April 24, 2018, https://www.wellandgood.com/brainwaves-biohack-sleep-health-focus/.

48   "Science of the Heart: Heart-Brain Communication," HeartMath, accessed September 26, 2023, https://www.heartmath.org/research/science-of-the-heart/heart-brain-communication/.

49   Joe Dispenza, *Becoming Supernatural: How Common People Are Doing the Uncommon*, 2nd ed. (Carlsbad, CA: Hay House), 52–53.

moment without making judgments."[50] Simply put, practicing meditation on a regular basis has helped us sleep better, be more productive, and ease our stress level. It is helpful in quieting the overactive mind.

Theta meditation is when you mentally disengage from your thoughts and start observing the images and symbols that show up from your subconscious. Your mind is completely relaxed and you're engaged in your inner world.

Achieving the theta state brings on the healing our minds and bodies are craving. With so many benefits, why not try to get to the theta state as often as possible? Making time for theta states throughout the day will help rejuvenate your mind and body, spark your creativity, and give you an energy boost.

Exercise
THETA MEDITATION

Working with a pendulum helps you reach that calm and relaxed theta state. Grab your pendulum and give it a try. Turn on soothing music, light a candle, shut the door, and engage with your pendulum. Rather than asking your pendulum questions, focus on your breath and let the pendulum move with your energy. Watch the pendulum move and notice your mind relaxing and letting go of the busy chatter. Allow the relaxation to set in while gazing at your moving pendulum. Keep breathing and notice what thoughts, information, or guidance are coming up. It may be a creative inspiration, a solution to a problem you're trying to solve, a reduction in your stress level, or another significant benefit. Journaling about what is coming up for you is a great way to capture your thoughts, feelings, and any downloads you receive. The theta state that your mind is experiencing with the help of the pendulum is a wonderful, healthy way to start or end your day, as well as to reset mid-day. Tune in to your own wisdom and universal intelligence as you enjoy a moment of peaceful bliss.

---

50   "Meditation and Mindfulness: What You Need to Know," National Center for Complementary and Integrative Health, National Institutes of Health, last modified June 2022, https://www.nccih.nih.gov/health/meditation-and-mindfulness-what-you-need-to-know.

STORY: AN AID IN MENTAL HEALTH AND WELLNESS

As we go deeper into our pendulum journey, we get the pleasure and joy of witnessing how these tools can be beneficial in healing. The Pride Institute provides the Minneapolis LGBTQ+ community with "an inclusive and accepting place for recovery through evidence-based treatment for substance abuse, sexual health and mental health."[51] *A friend, who has been a staff member at Pride for over a decade, believed that we had something of great value to offer the Pride clients. Here's a story of how we witnessed healing take place:*

When we arrived at Pride, we came prepared with handcrafted pendulums to donate to each client we were interacting with. The clients were thrilled to each receive a pendulum and learn how to work with it. We began our workshop with a grounding meditation, inviting each participant to let go of anything that was occupying their mind for the next hour and become fully present. After that, we got a chance to talk about our journey to pendulums and how we use them in our daily lives. Since we are both certified life coaches, working with this very vibrant, inquisitive community of clients was a natural fit. They were eager to learn and to try their new pendulums out for themselves.

Getting this large group of over thirty clients to connect with their pendulums was a complete joy. Their hearts were so open on their journey to recovery, and they were extremely excited to add this special tool, the pendulum, to their recovery toolkit. The look of amazement on their faces as they got to connect their energy to the pendulum and watch it move was an incredible gift to us. We believe that anyone who is open to using a pendulum will be able to connect with it. This group instantly took to them.

As our workshop continued, we practiced several techniques, including a demonstration of checking the chakras. We had willing volunteers who wanted to see if their chakras were open. If all seven chakras are open, your body's energy can flow freely. If there are blocks in any of the chakras, negative energy from trauma can get stuck in the body. Stuck energy can lead to illness and disease. The volunteers gave us permission to open their chakras that were blocked. It was informative and gratifying. Not to mention, it's something that all the workshop participants could start practicing at home on their journey to health.

---

51   Pride Institute, "Pride Institute Awarded Newsweek's Best Addiction Treatment Center Honor for a Second Year Running," September 18, 2021, https://pride-institute.com/wp-content/uploads/2023/02/Pride-Institute-Newsweek-Press-Release-2021-1.pdf.

When we left the Pride Institute, our hearts were full of love and gratitude for this community. They were very grateful that we showed up and shared our passion for pendulums, and they passed along notes of appreciation. We were even more thankful to them for trusting us with a small step on their healing journey.

Testing for Food Sensitivities

It's possible to determine what foods are optimal for you or whether you may have sensitivities to certain foods with the use of your AGA. Getting the right balance of nutrients is imperative to optimal health and wellness. Your pendulum taps into your body's inner knowing and can help guide your journey to healthy eating. You can start right now by going to your refrigerator and taking out the foods you typically eat. For example, grab some cheese out of your refrigerator, hold the pendulum over the cheese, and ask if it would be beneficial for your body to eat the cheese. Your body will literally tell you, as it knows on a cellular level what is good for it. You will see the pendulum swing in either a yes or a no motion. If it says no, ask if you may have a food sensitivity to that particular cheese. Be sure to then visit your primary care provider to discuss any health or food sensitivity issues you suspect you may have before beginning any self-led treatments or diets.

Another fun way to determine what foods are best for your body is to take your pendulum on a field trip to your local grocery store. If you don't mind getting a couple of stares, take out your pendulum and hold it over whatever food you're wanting to buy. Additionally, you can test whether a certain food is fresh or free of harmful chemicals. We personally love this method because people at the store around us are curious about what we're doing, which can lead to a spark of wonder in others. This, in turn, can guide them to discover something new about themselves, and we get to continue to share our message of wellness.

If you're not getting the answers you're seeking in a busy environment like a grocery store, keep in mind that there may be a lot happening in a busy place. Do not worry. Bring those groceries home and test them in the peace and quiet of your kitchen. Next time you go to the grocery store, come prepared with a list of all the foods that are beneficial for your body. Eventually, you'll end up with a refrigerator that is full of foods that bring you the most energy, vitality, and wellness. Again, if you do identify any food sensitivities, we encourage you to consult your healthcare practitioner for further testing and guidance.

Testing for allergies can be done similarly. You can start out by asking your pendulum to tell you if you have any allergies. It will show you a yes or no. If you have a hunch that you may have a specific allergy, such as to pollen, ask your pendulum to confirm. Keep asking questions to help you understand your body. Having these data points can help you determine how to take the next steps and work with a healthcare practitioner to optimize your environment and diet.

Pendulums for Healers

We often hear stories about what valuable and helpful tools pendulums are for those who work in the healing arts. We are fortunate to have many friends in the healing community and love to learn how pendulums help them navigate their daily life. Holistic medical practitioners may sometimes use a pendulum for making diagnoses and determining the most appropriate treatment for a patient's condition. This may be done by holding a pendulum over different parts of the body and learning how the pendulum responds. Using this method allows the practitioner to determine potential problematic locations in and on the body. When the problem is identified by scanning the body, the healer typically holds the pendulum over the problem area and activates the healing through intention. An example of a healing intention may be "I am restoring physical, mental, and emotional harmony for optimal health and wellness." Allowing the pendulum to move while repeating the intention begins the healing process. For optimal results, staying detached from the outcome and allowing adequate time for healing to take place is necessary by both the holistic practitioner and the patient. Expecting instant healing is not realistic. It is very important that both the practitioner and the patient are aligned in the intention and process used in the healing work. It may take time and multiple sessions, but having strong belief in positive outcomes is a crucial component of the process.[52]

The pendulum can also be used to determine which remedies to use by placing it over a selection of over-the-counter medications. It will give a posi-

---

52   Percy and Percy, *Pendulums for Guidance and Healing*, 96–97.

tive response to those that are most beneficial for the patient. Make sure to talk to your primary care provider first to confirm there are no contraindications with other medications you take.

Pendulums aren't just for holistic medical practitioners. Physicians trained in Western medicine have been known to source their intuition with the help of a pendulum as well. Anya is an in-patient psychiatrist who deals with patients everyday who are in mental health crises and are facing life-changing decisions. Handling difficult situations everyday requires her to stay grounded. Whether it is a personal question or one about how to approach a sensitive situation at work, a pendulum has become her trusted tool.

ANYA'S STORY

When I can't trust my gut and I'm torn about what's right for me, the pendulum has been a means of tapping into my inner wisdom. When I'm searching for answers in the wrong places, meaning outside of myself, I like having the ability to efficiently and quickly seek my answers with a tool at my fingertips that provides me peace of mind. We all hold the power to exercise our free will within ourselves, and this is simply a means of reaffirming that. From a professional point of view, I am a believer that we have the power to control our own destiny. One of my roles is to empower my patients and help them trust that they have the answers within.

Relationships

Relationships—the cornerstone of our existence. We are all meant to love and be loved. Love is the ultimate truth in our existence. Without getting too existential, we have all experienced the struggle of navigating relationships at one time or another. If you have not, rest assured, it *will* happen at some point. Using your pendulum to clarify and confirm what is right for you in your relationships is a profound way to ensure your life is in balance. The following are a few sample questions about where and how to begin exploring what is optimal for you. Whether you are in a romantic relationship, in a business partnership, or dealing with an issue with a friend or family member, it's refreshing to know that you can follow your heart to improve relationships as a result of your pendulum work. Here are some sample questions to get you started on enhancing the important relationships in your life.

- "Am I ready to find a romantic partner this year?" Adding a time frame is a good way to get specific.
- "Is [name of person] the most optimal partner for me at this point in my life? Are they the most optimal partner long-term?" Be careful with these types of questions, as they can be very subjective. Remember, it's all about how you frame up the question. Be as specific as possible.
- "Am I in love with [name of person]?"
- If you're newly dating someone, ask your pendulum if it's for your most optimal good to keep exploring the relationship. You might ask, "Is it in my best interest to go out with [name of person] again?" If you get a maybe, you could ask more questions, such as "Is [name of person] a trustworthy person?"
- If you're already in a committed relationship, you can ask questions about how to continue to strengthen the partnership. "Is it in my best interest to take the next step in my relationship with [name of person], to get engaged/married/move in together, etc.?" Or try "Will it benefit me to communicate to [name of person] how I feel about my relationship with them?"

It's crucial to keep your questions centered on yourself, not another person. You don't want to ask if a certain person is in love with you because you're not connected to their subconscious and don't know what they think or feel. Also, you can't control the outcome of their decisions. Keep the focus on yourself as the pendulum is connected to you and taps into *your* subconscious and inner wisdom, not that of someone else. By doing so, you're regulating your own feelings and actions from a place of self-agency. When you're ready, you can take the most optimal steps for your highest good. How empowering is that?

Julie is a single mom with three boys between the ages of six and thirteen. After battling illness and going through a divorce, Julie was looking for answers. She has used her pendulum in many cases when she needs guidance and to confirm what she truly wants: what is in her heart. She uses her pendulum mostly for the big questions to help her navigate her life, especially new relationships since her divorce.

JULIE'S STORY

I know that I have a really good head on my shoulders, but after my divorce, many things in my life were left out of alignment for me, especially when I found myself dating again after being married for thirteen years. As confident as I am, I didn't know I'd experience so many moments of insecurity and anxiety when I started developing feelings for someone new. When triggers would show up, I didn't know how to handle them.

One example of how I have used my pendulum to help me is when I went through breakups and I wanted to reach out to an ex but wasn't sure if I should. My heart told me one thing, and my head would tell me another. That's when I'd reach for my pendulum. What has been most profound is how quickly I'm able to move on by using my pendulum. When I'm pondering a situation, instead of ruminating and getting anxious, I go to my pendulum and get the clarity I need. It saves me from not getting stuck in my head, constantly overanalyzing, and questioning myself.

I'm at the point in my life where I like what I've built. I have listened to the guidance of my own intuition through my pendulum. It's always right, and I trust that I'm on the right path because I'm giving myself the right answer. Knowing that I have access to this information is golden. I trust that my intuition will continue to guide me through my pendulum work.

Business and Career

As cofounders of our joint businesses, we occasionally differ in our viewpoints and need to align on making optimal decisions. Pendulums are wonderful tools to help gain alignment. Many times, when making a decision for our business, we will both consult our own pendulums on the same question individually. Often, we end up getting the same answer, making it easy to act on it. It's that simple. It is a bit more complicated when we consult our own pendulums on the same question and get different answers. When you and your business partners, colleagues, team members, or anyone else you're working with (hopefully they are well versed in the use of the pendulum, just like you), are getting different answers from your intuition via your pendulum, then it is time to consider how both of you can compromise and still be in alignment.

One example is when we were putting together a proposal for a coaching engagement. We both had different points of view on how to price the project we were bidding on, and we each had very logical explanations why one of us wanted to go in with a high-cost bid, while the other one wanted to go in with a lower-cost bid. We ended up working with our pendulums to establish a price point that was acceptable to both the client and us. Not only did we feel good about our decision from a business standpoint, but we also felt good about it in our hearts. Because we were both willing to consult our intuition as part of the decision-making process in business, we both ended up feeling really great about the path we chose to move forward—and we won the job!

For many, our career is where we receive our sense of security, stability, and livelihood. Our work provides a sense of purpose and direction and has a large impact on our overall well-being. There's no doubt that career is a major component of life, just like relationships, health, spirituality, and finances.

You can apply your pendulum to help you navigate your career, and there are endless ways to put your AGA to work (no pun intended). Whether you are a stay-at-home caregiver, a corporate executive, a business owner, or a student, pendulums can become a daily companion in your personal life as well as your professional life.

The biggest career-related question that our clients ask us is if they are on the right career path. We have connected with many who struggle with this area of their lives and feel stuck in jobs they don't necessarily enjoy.

One example occurred when we had our pendulums for sale at an event in Minnesota. A group of young women approached us and were curious, so we gave them a tutorial and a mini pendulum coaching session. They were fascinated and began to test them out for themselves. One woman in particular was very drawn to a beautiful pendulum made of citrine and aventurine. We showed her how to calibrate it and she began working with it. This woman was a registered nurse but was having a tough time at work and was questioning whether she should leave her job. She began by asking the pendulum if she was in the right industry at that point in her life. The pendulum told her yes. She was surprised, as she felt disengaged at work and that her position as a nurse wasn't going as well as it had in the past. She admitted that she was discouraged, wanted something more, and had taken the MCAT exam to apply to medical school a few years ago.

She next asked if it was in her best interest to consult with her HR department. The answer came back as a no. "Hmmm, that's strange," she thought.

"Why not?" Next, she asked if she should talk to her boss about the challenges she was experiencing. The pendulum responded with a strong yes. Since she had been thinking about pursuing medical school years back, she asked the pendulum if she was in the right job for her at this time. She got a no. Next, she asked if the right path for her was to expand her career. A big yes. Her final question was whether it was in her best interest to explore medical school. Yes! She ended up purchasing the pendulum. The following week she let us know that she talked to her boss, who indicated that he'd been wanting to talk with her about a scholarship opportunity for one of his staff to continue their studies. She applied and was accepted into the program. She also ended up receiving the scholarship and mentorship she needed to pursue her path. Her pendulum helped her gain the clarity she needed to steer her toward a major life decision. And it happened in about ten minutes. Side note: the citrine and aventurine in the pendulum she ended up taking home are both wonderful stones for supporting career success.

Adding a layer of intuitive wisdom to decision-making for business ownership or your career is a wonderful way to help you enjoy your work every day. When you feel good about the decisions you make, you are more likely to follow through with them and realize all the benefits that result from those decisions. Sharon is a healer and a spiritual business owner. Her story is an example of leveraging intuitive guidance through the use of a pendulum and how it can lead to professional and personal success.

SHARON'S STORY

It wasn't until later in my journey that I became overly curious about pendulums. Oddly, I was a bit intimidated as much as amazed at the idea of crystals and divination tools. My nearly adult daughter was the first to give me a pendulum, and she told me that it had just jumped out at her when she was thinking which one would be best for me.

As I started into my new life opening my sound, light, and energy center and bringing the Harmonic Egg into the Twin Cities market, I often found myself reaching for the pendulum that my daughter had given me. I utilized it for everything from business decisions to figuring out what sound healing sessions to put myself on in the Harmonic Egg. I had intuitive clarity for others and what they needed when they came into the center. However, I found that

I struggled with knowing the right session for myself, so I'd frequently consult with my pendulum. Since working with my pendulum on a regular basis, I have learned to unwind negative energy, clear my field, forecast, and so much more.

Finances

Using your pendulum to help you figure out how to invest your money is always an option that is available to you. Whether you're evaluating what stocks or mutual funds to invest in, establishing a money market account for yourself, or just opening a savings account at your local bank, checking in with your intuition is always a good idea. This information is not intended to be a substitute for working with your financial professional, but it is an extra step that can really get you aligned on planning and achieving your financial goals and objectives.

When deciding where you want to invest your hard-earned dollars, it is always important to capture your financial objectives. Are you saving up for a down payment on a house? Are you starting a 529 plan to save for your child's college education? Do you have multiple priorities, such as short-term, less risky investments or long-term investments where you can take more financial risk?

Clarify what you want to accomplish. If you are identifying which financial planner to work with, we suggest that you talk to several. Learn about their investment philosophies and their approach to managing your money. When you are narrowing down which investment professional to work with, that is when your intuition can be a fantastic guide. Working with your pendulum, narrow down the options to which professional is most optimal to manage your money based on your goals and objectives. If you are getting a no on all the financial professionals that you've interviewed, that means that you haven't found the right one. Keep going and meet with others. Your discovery process will eventually lead you to the right professional partner.

When it comes to investing your money, you want to make sure that the person entrusted with the task checks all the boxes—education, philosophy, experience, results, values, personality, and energy. You'll be able to better achieve your goals and objectives when you feel confident that you have chosen the right advisor to partner with.

The same philosophy and process can apply to other professional relationships. If you are in the process of buying or selling a home or finding your perfect apartment, it is imperative that you have a fantastic relationship with your real estate agent. Feeling confident in your agent's skills and abilities is key to your inner peace through a stressful time. Your agent is going to be negotiating on your behalf, and you want this person to always have your best interests at heart. Your intuitive guidance, shown to you by your pendulum, will lead you to picking the right agent for the job.

After you pick the right professional and start your search for a new home or apartment, don't forget to bring your pendulum on your house-hunting or apartment-touring journey. Homes hold energy, and you want to make sure that you are energetically aligned with a home that you are considering purchasing or renting. Work with your pendulum by asking simple questions, such as "Is this an optimal home for me and my family?" Your intuition will let you know. Choosing a home that checks all the boxes of what you're looking for is a wonderful feeling. Don't settle for anything less.

Prioritizing

Most of us have multiple competing priorities every day. Sometimes it's a challenge knowing what will be the most useful task to spend our time on. You can determine your priority list each day with the help of a pendulum. Doing this quick check-in is a surefire way to clarify what to focus on. This is a great exercise that can be applied to many areas of your life. And the best part is that it's quick and easy.

When you sit down in the morning to make your daily to-do list, take a moment to review this list with your pendulum. Both of us often tend to make long lists of everything we have to accomplish in a day. That feeling when you look at your list of all the tasks is another cause of stress in our lives. Why not use the pendulum to check in and see what items on your list really need to be done that day? We often find that 30 to 40 percent of everything that ends up on the to-do list is not really necessary. Plus, it's really simple to do. After calibrating your pendulum, follow these steps:

1. Hold the pendulum on top of the item you've written down on your to-do list and ask, "Is it optimal for me to focus on this item today?" You will quickly get a yes or no answer.

2. Follow these directions for all the items on your to-do list and cross off all the items that you get a no answer for. Notice how your to-do list just got shorter?

3. Take a good look at what you have left on your list. Does it make sense why the items that weren't really critical to get done today are crossed off?

4. Breathe a big sigh of relief and focus on what is left on your list. Now take a few minutes to prioritize your shortened to-do list with the help of your pendulum.

5. Hold the pendulum over the remaining items one by one and ask, "Is it optimal for me to complete this task first?" If you get a no answer, ask, "Is it optimal for me to complete this task second?" Keep asking until you get a yes answer and continue this prioritization exercise until you have an optimal order for all the things you need to accomplish. It may seem like a lot of work, but once you get the hang of it, you'll finish optimizing your to-do list in a few minutes.

The most amazing part of using a pendulum to cut down and prioritize your to-do list is noticing how nicely your day flows. When you follow your intuition about how to structure your day, you'll quickly realize that your productivity will increase. You'll get through your to-do list much faster, and you'll have so much more fun crossing items off your list. Of course, things may come up during the day that take you away from a productive state of flow. If you catch yourself straying from your original plan, pause for a moment and check in using your pendulum. Don't get flustered; reprioritize and flow with it.

Finding Missing Objects

When you can't remember where you placed your keys or any other missing object, the pendulum is a fast and easy solution for assistance. You'll be shocked at how easy it is and how much time you save by using your pendulum to find missing objects. We'll walk you through a couple of different methods.

Map Method

1. Draw a simple blueprint of your home or the space where you are looking. Please don't focus on the artistry of your drawing. A simple representation is all you need.

2. Next, after calibrating your pendulum, hold it over each room and ask, "Is the [object] located in the [room] right now?" You can do this room by room until you get a yes answer.

3. If you think you've lost something outside of your home, try using a map to ask questions and narrow your search area.

Question Method

Asking the pendulum where you've buried that old album or any other item you're looking for is simple and quick.

1. Start broad by asking if the object is in the house, car, garage, etc.

2. Next, begin narrowing in on where the object is hiding. While your rational mind has forgotten where it is, your subconscious knows since you placed it there in the first place. So you can ask questions such as "Is the [object] on the lower level of the house at this moment? Is it in the basement? It is in the master bedroom?"

3. Once you've narrowed in on a space in the house, begin asking questions such as "Is the [object] in the right side of the room? Is it on the left side of the room? When you've narrowed it down, begin asking more questions. "Is the [object] in the closet? Is it on the top half?" It's so fun to find what's been missing!

KARINA'S STORY

Here's a quick story that happened to Karina that demonstrates the versatility and everyday magic that can happen when you engage your pendulum in daily life.

My adult kids are not big gamers, but when they are visiting home, occasionally they enjoy playing Xbox. When my younger son was home from college on fall break, he couldn't find his Xbox anywhere in the house. I searched and searched and couldn't find it either. I stopped searching and just forgot that it was lost. Right before coming home for the long holiday break, my son reminded me that his Xbox was still nowhere to be found and asked me to look for it.

When I had a quiet moment to myself, I did what any logical person would do to find a lost object—I asked my pendulum! Since I was the one who put it away months before, I knew the answer was buried somewhere deep in my subconscious mind. Here's the process that I used:

I asked the pendulum if the Xbox was in the house and got a yes.

I narrowed down the options of where it was by asking the pendulum if the Xbox was on the second floor of my house and got a no. Then I asked if the Xbox was on the main level of my house and got a yes.

I took my pendulum into every room of the main level of my house and kept asking if the Xbox was in this room. I kept getting nos until I entered the family room and finally got a yes.

I kept walking around the family room, asking my pendulum whether the Xbox was in this or that part of the room. When I approached the TV, I finally got a yes from the pendulum. I moved the TV and saw that nothing was behind it but some cords. Then I opened the cabinet underneath the TV, and sure enough, there was the Xbox on the bottom shelf, facing backward. We probably looked there a bunch of times in the past for it but thought it was an old DVR with cords sticking out of it, facing backward.

I quickly texted my son a pic of the Xbox. He was very pleased. I'm so grateful that I trust this amazing tool to work quickly and easily with my intuition and get the information out that helps me move my life forward in an optimal way.

Travel

Whether for work or fun, travel requires many decisions. Where will my family, friends, or I have the most enjoyable time? What dates are best to travel? What clothes do I need to pack? How do I schedule my itinerary once my destination is decided? Who is the best travel agent to work with? The questions are endless.

We've found that the pendulum is just the tool needed to help. This AGA can help you decide on anything and everything travel related. And it's completely portable! Your pendulum can also help you bond with the energy of new locations, bringing in a sense of adventure and connection with new lands, cultures, and experiences. We love ethically sourcing materials and unique pieces for our pendulums from different parts of the world when we travel. The vibrations of these pieces are felt far and wide, and they are genuine reminders that we are all one and connected. Here are a few ideas on how to work with your pendulum for travel success.

Travel Planning

Are you beginning to plan for a family vacation but not sure where to go? Try grabbing a map and holding your pendulum over various countries and cities. Look for where your pendulum gives you a yes movement. Once you have several locations, write them down on a piece of paper and ask your pendulum questions about which locations are most optimal for you and your family to travel to. Keep narrowing them down until you find your perfect destination.

If you have a location picked out, use your pendulum to help you select which sites to see. Or perhaps you're planning a beach getaway and would like to know which hotel is the best fit for you and your travel companions?

Maybe you have a work trip coming up and you'd like to get to know the destination city a little better. You can work with your pendulum to help select the attractions worth visiting. Pull up the city guide and narrow down your search by asking your pendulum which attractions are optimal to visit.

We've found that our pendulums are instrumental when we travel in terms of feeling the energy and connection of a new location. We've had some mystical experiences with our pendulums while traveling, especially in areas that are known to have powerful energy vortexes. Two such locations have been in Sedona, Arizona, and at the Stonehenge heritage site in England.

LANA'S STONEHENGE STORY

While on a family trip to London, we decided to take a day trip to Stonehenge, a dream come true for me since I studied anthropology and am fascinated with ancient civilizations. It was a typical cold and blustery day in England, and we set out early in the morning. Upon arrival at the site, I could feel an enormous shift in the energy. It felt downright powerful, like the ancestors were all around us, guarding the site and signaling for those who were receptive to their spirit to work with them. Stonehenge is the meeting place of fourteen different ley lines, making it one of the most powerfully charged energy vortexes in the world. Energy vortexes can have certain spiritual properties associated with them and can be highly conductive of spiritual actions, such as prayer, meditation, and healing.

My intuition directed me to take out my pendulum and see what would happen. I'm not one to ignore this kind of calling, and despite the cold, I did just that. My pendulum started moving in a clockwise direction, more wildly than usual. For me, this direction indicates positive energy being ushered in. I closed my eyes and had a moment.

During my brief meditation with my pendulum swinging, I received a download. I was to make a special edition collection of Stonehenge pendulums using Preseli bluestone, the very same stone that the inner circle of Stonehenge is built from. This rare stone is only found in the Preseli Hills of Wales in the United Kingdom, about 150 miles from Stonehenge. Preseli bluestone has been known for its deeply grounding energy and magical, healing properties. I decided to follow this guidance and purchased Preseli bluestone beads from the site's gift shop.

I decided that the special edition collection would feature five pendulums. Creating the Stonehenge line of pendulums was a spiritual experience. Preseli bluestone is said to embody an ancient vibration and assist with connecting with the energy of past lives. I was elated to connect these beautiful and magical pendulums to the souls that they belong with in this lifetime.

What unfolded next was very puzzling and magical. The first two women who purchased the pendulums in the Stonehenge Collection had visceral reactions when they first saw and held their pendulums. It's as if they were being called to the healing energies of Stonehenge, and while they didn't know each other, I couldn't help but wonder if they were meant to have these pendulums as some kind of connection point. At the time of this writing, they have not met ... yet! Here are their stories.

DAWN'S STORY

Doesn't it fill you with wonder when someone or something comes into your life in ways that change you at a core level? My women's self-empowerment organization was a participant in an event in Minneapolis. After setting up my table, I strolled through the room to connect with other participants. And there were Lana and Karina. I was filled with joy to see the two of them—and their pendulums!

We hugged and laughed as we spent time catching up. Lana told me about her trip to Stonehenge and how inspired she'd been while there. She mentioned how experiencing Stonehenge had led her to create pendulums inspired by powerful energy as she walked among the sacred, mysterious stone giants.

At their event table, resplendent with magnificent pendulums resting on plush velvet, there was a pendulum behind the standing display near the back of their table. I felt its energy before even seeing it. Lana reverently picked it up, showed it to me, and gently placed it in my hands. She and Karina told me how this pendulum had come into being, inspired by Lana's time at Stonehenge. The pendulum is called Ancestral Wisdom. What followed next, for me, was nothing short of a miracle.

In 2016, I traveled to India and spent twenty-one days in silence, being taught by enlightened monks. Our twelve-hour days were filled with meditation, chanting in Sanskrit, eating specially prepared meals, and choosing not to talk at all (so we could do the inner work of healing, expanding, and walking in the direction of enlightened living). Though I walked a spiritual and self-discovery path since childhood, I'd never experienced anything that had catapulted me into such depth and transformation as my time there did. It positively changed me forever.

For the first fifteen or sixteen days of my experience in India, the monks skillfully and lovingly led us into the depths of our very beings. We dove deep into past hurts, explored who we are as humans, and learned about karma and other ancient teachings. Through it all, we began a purifying, a cleansing, a letting-go of the heavy baggage we can carry throughout our lives. We felt lighter, more present and loving—both toward ourselves and toward others. The preparation was complete, and then the big day came.

We were ceremoniously led onto the upper floor of the 8,000-person temple, which is reserved for sacred processes. It was an honor to be there. The space was gently lit by hundreds of candles and the fragrance of special oils wafted into our noses as sacred music played gently in the background. We each took our place and were led through the final steps of our awakening and enlightenment.

At one point, near the end of the ceremony, my inner being began to swirl in a profound radiance. Tears ran down my cheeks and I felt new, alive in a way I'd never experienced. My senses were keen and my heart beat with love. The spiraling, swirling sensation in my body continued, and when I walked outside the temple and saw the moon, it was as though I was seeing it for the first time.

I experienced oneness with flowers, many closing their petals for the evening, pulsating with life and beauty. Our evening meal, presented with love and care, landed on my tongue with the freshness of the young tastebuds of a child.

Though the spiraling, swirling, radiant divine energy I'd experienced at the top of the temple began to cease, I continued to feel its effects. I longed to feel that same swirling energy again, and since my time in the temple, it's happened very few times and usually without the same intensity. And then I met the pendulum Ancestral Wisdom on that day with Lana and Karina. Simply by holding the pendulum, I felt the feeling return with the same intensity as the evening in the temple. I was shocked!

The Ancestral Wisdom pendulum is more than a sacred object to me, though that alone would be lovely! She is a friend, a reminder of the inner wisdom I hold within me. Ancestral Wisdom supports me to quickly come to that higher place in my soul, that true part of my being. Though my connection with her allows me to tap into my soul for answers to questions and provides me with guidance, I received another gift that I hadn't expected.

When I was a little girl, infused with the teachings of Catholicism (which I've since replaced with wider spiritual beliefs), I had a few mystical experiences while holding a pink crystal rosary my grandmother Rosie had given me.

Along with the many benefits I receive from my Ancestral Wisdom pendulum, she provides me with an amplified version of my little-girl-rosary mysticism and awakens the swirling, radiant energy I experienced in the temple in India. As I hold her in my hand right now, I feel great joy and appreciation. She is never far from my side.

DEE'S STORY

I believe that each pendulum chooses us for a reason, and it is our responsibility to discover that reason.

When Lana posted a picture of herself at Stonehenge with a beautiful pendulum, something inside me stirred. I felt an immediate connection to the piece, as if it resonated with the very essence of my being. Now, as I hold it in my hand, I can feel the tingling sensation, and even speaking about it gives me goosebumps. But there is more to it than that.

As if by magic, Lana had an appointment near my home the very next day and was able to deliver the Stonehenge pendulum to me in person. It was as if destiny had orchestrated this meeting, as if she was meant to experience the energy in my home—a space that feels like a portal, brimming with vibrant energy. When Lana left, she left with a sense of invigoration, describing herself as charged in a positive, uplifting way. For me, this space in my home always felt mystical, and Lana confirmed it. I feel like the pendulum is connected to this portal and that is why Lana was meant to experience it firsthand.

This pendulum is unlike anything I've ever encountered. Its uniqueness and transformative power became apparent from the moment it came into my home. I cleared and infused the Stonehenge pendulum with reiki blessings. From that point forward, I kept it close to me at all times, meditating with it and forming a deep bond. This extraordinary piece emits such a unique and powerful energy, which resonates within me, flowing through every fiber of my being.

The following day brought another synchronicity—my family would be traveling to London in a few months, and, of course, I would visit Stonehenge. But why now? What is the significance of this trip and the pendulum? I once lived in England and visited Stonehenge in my youth, yet I sense that I am being called back for a reason.

During my meditations, I sought guidance about the Stonehenge pendulum. Each time, the answer resounded within me—"Yes, this pendulum is meant for me!" It carries a message and holds a purpose. I sense a connection to the land, to our beautiful planet. My calling is to work with the land, to aid in its healing, and to guide others in utilizing it wisely.

Pendulums and Pets

We are big fans of our pets. Lana has two Siberian huskies and Karina has a mini goldendoodle. For many of us, our furry companions are key additions to our families and are the source of much love and happiness. It's no doubt that we want to care for them and ensure their most optimal health and well-being. Your pendulum is a powerful tool to learn more about your animal(s) and their needs. It's also fairly measurable, which is helpful to understanding how much of something they need or how long an injury might take to heal. Using charts can be very helpful when working with animals since your furry friend most likely can't talk.

There are various ways you can use your pendulum to help understand what your pet needs. You can connect with your pet to learn more about what is ailing them. If your pet is not acting like himself, is tired and lethargic, or simply doesn't look well, grab your pendulum and try the exercises that follow. Use your superpower—your intuition—to assist you. Once you receive answers, it's always best to err on the side of caution and pay a visit to your veterinarian to ask for their expert advice on what your pet may need.

The examples used in this book are for informational purposes only and do not constitute providing medical advice or professional services. The information provided should not be used for diagnosing or treating a health problem or disease, and those seeking personal medical advice for their pets should consult with a licensed veterinarian. Always seek the advice of your veterinarian regarding your pet's medical condition.

Pet Pendulum Calibration

Calibrating a pendulum with your pet strengthens the connection of the pet with the pendulum. Here are the steps to do so:

1. Get grounded and state your intention and source from where you're receiving your answers.
2. Hold your pendulum over your pet's body, either on the back or the tummy. If you have a pet pendulum, attach it to a longer chain.
3. Ask the pendulum to please show you what yes looks like for [pet name].
4. Ask the pendulum to please show you what no looks like for [pet name].

After going through these steps, you can begin asking questions about your pet. You can also scan the pet's body to see where internal problems might be located. Hold the pendulum over various points of the pet's body and pay attention to where the pendulum swings. From there, you'll be able to tell if there's an issue that needs to be addressed by a vet. The pendulum may swing in your yes or no movement, clockwise, or counterclockwise. If you're not clear what each motion indicates, ask your pendulum to clarify the movement for you.

Here's an example of what that might look like:

- "Is it right for me to believe that [pet name] is having digestive problems at this time?" If you receive a yes ...
- "Are the digestive issues that [pet name] is experiencing caused by the food he is currently eating?" If you receive a no ...
- "Are the digestive problems that [pet name] is experiencing due to something he ate outside while at the park?" If you receive a yes ...
- "Is it right for me to believe that it's best to use a moonstone with [pet name]?"
- Keep asking questions that you are curious about in relation to your pet.

You can then act accordingly. Follow the calibration steps, and try some energy work on your own. In the meantime, always connect with your veterinarian to determine the best direction forward for your pet. There is much to know about energy work with pets. We love using our pendulums to help us answer basic questions we have about our pets. However, it's really helpful and recommended to work with a pet energy professional for this kind of work.

Identifying Crystals to Support Your Pet's Needs

If you are knowledgeable in using crystals to heal yourself, the same crystals may be used to support your pet. Healing crystals can help with a multitude of conditions, including aggression, fear, anxiety, attachment, shyness, excessive barking, dealing with change, trauma, and digestive issues such as an upset stomach. Let the crystals work their magic by releasing their healing properties. Your pet will absorb the energy.

Our favorite way to incorporate a crystal into our pets' lives is to use a pendulum with a healing crystal attached. We make pendulums for pets, which are smaller and can either be attached to an interchangeable pendulum or attached to your pet's collar, depending on the size of the animal and your comfort level with this. Read on to learn which are some of our favorite go-to crystals and how to work with pet pendulums.

Rose Quartz

Rose quartz is the crystal of unconditional love. Its calming properties ease frustration and nervous tension, bring comfort in stressful situations, and radiate feelings of security and peace. If your furry friend is a rescue, rose quartz can help heal any past trauma and allow for a greater connection. If your pet is tense or shy when meeting new people, rose quartz will help your pet learn how to accept love and companionship. It also helps dissipate fear, replacing it with feelings of confidence and love. As an added bonus, it can help decrease muscle tension and speed up healing from physical injuries. For pets who struggle with frustration and irritability, a rose quartz crystal is sure to help.

Amethyst

Amethyst is the ultimate healer, as it remedies both physical and emotional pain that your pet may be suffering from. If your pet lacks energy, amethyst will give her a boost of energy needed to play and run happily. Amethyst crystals are a must if you have an older cat or dog. Our dogs have been able to shift into a state of calm after stressful situations with the help of an amethyst. This stone has served as an ally with helping our pets relax by infusing a calming effect.

Clear Quartz

If you're looking for a crystal to improve the overall health of your pet, clear quartz is a great choice. Clear quartz helps clear negative energies, creates a sense of calm, and increases your pet's confidence when interacting with others. This healing crystal can also help reduce excessive barking or aggressiveness. Clear quartz is an amplifier, meaning, it can help your pet with any intention. So if there is a specific area where your pet needs healing or an emotion that needs uplifting, set an intention with your clear quartz and watch it work its magic.

Moonstone

Moonstone brings nurturing, soothing energy to help with your dog's healing process after traumatic experiences. Considered a "stone for new beginnings," it's an excellent crystal for pets post-surgery, after moving into a new home, or if you've just brought a pet home from a shelter. If your pet is impulsive or reactive, its gentle, soothing energies can stabilize emotions and reduce nervous tension, bringing a relaxed vibe into your dog's environment. Moonstone aids the digestive system, so if your pet is having stomach issues, it can help eliminate toxins and fluid retention as well as degenerative conditions of the skin, fur, and eyes.

Citrine

Known as the stone of joy and happiness, citrine energizes all aspects of life. It raises self-esteem and self-confidence and stimulates the brain. If your pet struggles with shyness or is lethargic, try a citrine crystal to promote motivation and balance emotions. Pets who exhibit symptoms of depression, fear, and separation anxiety will benefit from its ability to assist in positive enthusiasm.

Cleansing and Charging Your Pet's Crystals

There are many ways to cleanse crystals and gemstones. When you first bring your pet's crystal home and again whenever needed, cleanse it with smoke or leave it in the moonlight, especially during a full moon. For more details, see chapter 4 for how to cleanse and charge your pendulum.

Whether it's soothing your pet's separation anxiety, calming hyperactivity, easing joint pain, or enhancing your emotional bond, a pet pendulum crystal can help your pet's healing. It is effective, natural, easy, and convenient. Using your pendulum for energy healing or attaching a pet pendulum to your pet's collar (if it's safe to do so) is a surefire way to naturally enhance your furry pal's overall well-being and foster a special connection between you and your pets.

SKY AND LANA'S STORY

When I saw Sky on Petfinder, a website that matches dogs with potential owners for adoption, I did a double take. I don't know why; he just caught my eye, and I knew that I had to inquire about him. At that point, I was poking around Petfinder, but I wasn't necessarily ready or serious about adopting a dog on my own.

Sky came home with me two days later. He was nine months and a typical rambunctious husky puppy. It was quite the transition, but I loved my new role as dog mom. My son was overjoyed, and my partner, who had dogs in the past, was a huge help.

At around one and a half years old, we noticed a lesion of some sort forming on his chin. It didn't get better after a few weeks and began to increase in size. It kept getting worse, and before we knew what was happening, it had spread to the area above one of his eyes. We didn't know what to do. The vet visits and bills began to pile up, but we were committed to figuring out what was wrong with him. His adorable face was overshadowed by these awful-looking lesions that were eroding his fur. And we didn't know if he was in pain. He didn't seem to be and rarely itched it.

For the next year, we bounced around from vet to vet trying to understand what was wrong. It was determined that it could be a zinc deficiency, and we were referred to a veterinarian who had experience caring for sled-dogs and knew the husky breed. We began seeing her regularly, running tests, and trying various medications and topical creams. This didn't help our relationship with Sky, as applying the creams required us to constantly be in Sky's face.

After another year, we were told by our vet that there wasn't anything more they could do to help us figure it out. They also indicated that the issue was most likely an autoimmune disease. We were then referred to a veterinary dermatologist to run more tests and see if this was the case. We were devastated. An autoimmune disease meant it could be fatal. I made the appointment right away and got in with the dermatological vet the following week.

At that point, Sky was taking a zinc supplement, but that was it. We had tried several kinds of medications, including various steroids to reduce the inflammation and clear up the lesions. The side effects were terrible! Sky ballooned into a chubby husky, which made it hard for him to run and play like he used to. The steroid also made him extremely thirsty. He guzzled water like he'd just crossed the desert all day every day. This caused him to urinate frequently, and he began having accidents at night. For about a year, we had to get up in the middle of the night, sometimes twice, to let him out to go to the bathroom. It was like having a newborn!

In the week prior to his big appointment with the dermatological vet, I sat with my pendulum for guidance. I had a hunch that he wasn't getting enough zinc, and I was distraught over the news that it was likely that he had an autoimmune disease. I asked if Sky needed more zinc. I got a strong yes. I also asked if Sky had an autoimmune disease. I received a strong no. What? But the vet indicated that's what it most likely was, and I trusted her. That wasn't the answer I was expecting, but it sure put my mind at ease a little. Based on the information that I received, I began giving Sky another dose of zinc, even though we hadn't seen the vet yet. I knew that it couldn't hurt him to have more zinc for a week.

The next week, we took Sky to the dermatological vet who ran the tests. The results? He needed more zinc, and it wasn't an autoimmune disease. I couldn't believe it! My intuition wasn't wrong, even about something like this. Somewhere over the two-year period that we had been running around from vet to vet, I had been reading about what the problem could be and learning about zinc deficiencies in dogs. My subconscious was storing all this information. In my case, I would have taken Sky to the vet either way—no questions asked. I am in no way knowledgeable enough to diagnose my dog. But the fact that what I knew deep down inside to be true was confirmed by a vet was jaw-dropping to me.

I am glad to report that Sky is much better today. He will be on a zinc supplement for life but is a happy boy. We've since adopted another husky, and I am finally living my childhood dream to have a dog (or two). I am so grateful that I was able to work with my pendulum to put my mind at ease and help me navigate how to best care for our beloved Sky.

Chapter 7
TROUBLESHOOTING

It doesn't matter if you're holding a pendulum for the first time or you're a seasoned pendulum pro. There might be times when your pendulum does not move or is swinging erratically. What if it stops working all together? What if your pendulum breaks? These are all good questions. Let's troubleshoot!

The following are a few reasons why you may need take a step back:

You may not be in the right headspace. Your higher self knows when you're ready. You may think you are, but your higher self knows what is best for you. Put the pendulum down and try again when you're feeling clearer and more grounded. At the very least, spend a few hours away from your pendulum. Calm your mind and body by relaxing, taking a nap, enjoying a hot bath, or spending time in nature. Exercise is another great way to reset yourself. When you are feeling rejuvenated, calm, and peaceful, you can get back to your pendulum session.

Your pendulum isn't calibrated properly. We always recommend that every time you sit down for a pendulum session, you take a moment to calibrate your pendulum for your yes, no, maybe, and not now movements. Additionally, we recommend that you start your session by asking a few questions that you already know the answers to, such as "Did I drink coffee this morning?" Starting your session with this simple practice sets you up for a successful session with confidence. When you are clear and comfortable with how the pendulum moves for you, you'll receive great comfort in the answers that you seek.

You're sick. Avoid using the pendulum during a time when you're not feeling well. Take time to rest and heal your body. Drink lots of water to stay hydrated. Come back to it when you're feeling better.

You are uncomfortable or are sitting with a poor posture. Make sure you're in a comfortable position when working with your pendulum. A desk or a table is ideal. You can rest the elbow of your dominant hand on the table if that is comfortable for you. Use a pillow behind your back if that helps you sit up straight.

Your environment is too chaotic. Are you using your pendulum while your family is buzzing all around you and distracting your focus? There's a good chance that your pendulum will still work just fine in a busy space. However, if you have the option to be in a quiet place where you and your pendulum can connect on a deep level, this is where you'll find the best results. If you have a sacred space dedicated to your meditation or energy work, this is likely the optimal place to work with your pendulum, especially if you are resolving major issues. Keep in mind that if you end up working with your pendulum in a chaotic environment, the crystals on your pendulum will absorb the energy of the place. Be sure to clear and charge your pendulum afterward.

You're skeptical about pendulum work. Believing in the power of the pendulum as a tool that connects with your intuition is key. If you don't believe that the pendulum is a tool that connects with your subconscious and energy, guess what? It won't. Someone who is open and receptive to working with a pendulum will get much better results. If you are a skeptic, we encourage you to learn more about this ancient practice and try it when you are ready.

The timing is off. If you are in a hurry, the pendulum may be picking up on your rushed energy. We encourage you to set aside time for your pendulum practice. Using your daily calendar to schedule daily time to connect with your pendulum will help you honor the practice. Daily pendulum practice will surely lead you to great insights about yourself and help you gain confidence in your decision-making.

Your pendulum has stored stagnant energy or someone else handled it. It may be as simple as cleansing and charging your pendulum. It's simple to store your pendulum with selenite when you are not using it. We also recommend that you give your pendulum gratitude, care, love, and respect. Honoring this tool will bring you optimal results. Take care of it and it will absolutely take care of you!

You may have energetic imbalances or blocks that need to be addressed. This happens. We all have energetic blocks from time to time, sometimes daily. Work with a friend or a partner to open your chakras (see page 93) and allow your energy to flow freely. Of course, you can do this for yourself too. Wait a few hours and try again.

It's not your perfect pendulum. Sometimes, it's simply not the right pendulum for you. Try another pendulum that appeals to you. Experiment with various shapes, weights, and crystals. Have faith that your perfect pendulum will find you. We have seen this happen so many times. Picking a pendulum is a fun, joyful experience. Do not get stressed out about it. Just believe!

It's time to replace your pendulum. On numerous occasions, we encounter people who tell us that their pendulum somehow "disappeared." There's a strong possibility that they misplaced their pendulum; however, we believe that pendulums can have a mind of their own. It's likely that the work that needed to happen with that particular pendulum is done and it's time to replace it. In addition, as mentioned before, the crystals in pendulums can become stagnant. Like any other tool, pendulums can also have a shelf life. Depending on how well you care for your pendulum, it can wear down. Energetically, you simply may be ready for a new one. When this is felt on a vibrational level, the pendulum may stop working as well for you.

You need a separate pendulum for a different purpose. Your pendulum is an extremely personal tool. Once you are connected with your pendulum and it is connected with your energy, it should not be shared with others. If you're a practitioner who works in the healing arts especially, your personal pendulum may not be the best choice to use with others, as it's working with your energy, not that of someone else. We recommend a separate pendulum or two for your clients. If you're sharing your personal pendulum with a curious friend, that's okay on occasion. However, know that it might not be as effective afterward for you. In this case, cleansing and charging it is wise. This should restore it back to its original state.

Your pendulum breaks. This is an interesting topic. Sometimes, people carry their pendulums in a purse or bag, and it ends up being tossed around. Over time, this can wear the pendulum down, and it can break. It's important to take good care of your pendulum. If you're going to carry it with you (and we suggest that you do since you never know when you're going to need advice and clarity), do so in a protective pouch or container. Make sure it's surrounded by something soft to cushion it. Infrequently, a pendulum simply breaks without explanation. In a case like this, one possibility is that the pendulum has taken a "hit" for you or was protecting you from something. It is believed that the pendulum's work is done.

Troubleshooting Summary

Working with a pendulum depends on how well you're able to connect to your inner wisdom. While living a high-vibe life all the time would be utopian, let's be real—as humans we simply don't always feel at our best. Being in the right frame of mind is important to letting the energy flow freely when working with your pendulum. However, even when you're not in the most optimal frame of mind, with practice and patience, you can work with your pendulum in your time of need. Try doing a grounding meditation or visualization exercise to move into a better head space. If you're feeling really low, keep in mind that you most likely won't go from one extreme to the other after one grounding exercise. Aim to raise your vibration up a few notches on the emotional scale back to a neutral state. Just feeling slightly better can help.

Also, remember to focus on your questions. Don't multitask while you're working with your pendulum. Connecting with your heart and your mind is necessary to be successful. If you don't believe and trust, your higher self already knows this, and ultimately this could be the biggest inhibitor for you. Your relationship with your pendulum should be one that is in harmony, so make sure you trust in the process and, most importantly, have fun and enjoy it!

CONCLUSION

Pendulums are more than a tool used to look within for answers. To us, they represent much more. For centuries, they have been revered for their accuracy, simplicity of use, and effectiveness by spiritual and cultural leaders, scientists, shamans, energy healers, and many others across the globe. This small, beautiful tool, often mistaken for a piece of jewelry, exemplifies a larger shift that is happening on a global scale. This shift is a journey within us.

Much like meditation, pendulums can help calm the mind and offer a temporary escape from the outside world. When we find a quiet place, get grounded, and begin our pendulum work, our minds start to shift to a state of deep and focused attention. When used with loving intentions, the pendulum can become an instrumental tool for overall mind-body well-being. Getting into a meditative state using a pendulum helps lower brain waves and turn down the mental noise. Learning to let go, surrender, and let your inner wisdom guide you to answers allows you to begin to align with what is truly authentic and meaningful for you. And when you live your life from a place of authenticity, life becomes smoother, more joyful, and more connected. Letting your ego, the controlling aspect of yourself that wants to always be right, step aside and receive what is for your optimal good without being attached to the outcome is the HeartCentric approach.

We hope this book inspired you to learn more about the pendulum and has taken you on a journey of exploration deep within your soul. Our mission is to bring awareness about this tool to as many as possible so that everyone can live their most optimal life and assist with a larger transformation already happening collectively. Our greatest wish is that each and every person reading this book will find their way to their most authentic truth with a pendulum, and by doing so, they will transform their life for the better and create a ripple effect. When we live in our joy, we feel more connected to ourselves, others, and the world. Ultimately, this is what will help our collective consciousness continue to shift into a New Earth.

Pendulums create a gateway to the heart and soul within each of us. The answers that we seek are already inside us, waiting to be unearthed through our intuition. They are our guides that help us slow down, connect, and start noticing the magic all around us. Having a personal amazing guidance assistant dedicated to you comes with benefits, the most important being that it leads you down only the right path—your own. This book only scratches the surface of the endless possibilities and uses for a pendulum. If you're curious to go deeper, we invite you to join us on our journey as we continue to explore the unlimited potential of how to use a pendulum to live your best life. Find us at hcdivinecreations.com.

$\mathcal{A}$ppendix
PENDULUM PRACTICES

The following charts and exercises are designed to help you as you develop your intuition and pendulum practice. We encourage you to have fun with these exercises, explore, and personalize your own practice. Don't get discouraged if it's taking some time to fine-tune your practice. Remember, like any other muscle you're trying to strengthen, your regimen will require some dedication and patience. Stay open and curious to the guidance you're receiving, and most importantly, trust yourself. You've got this!

$\mathcal{P}$ercentage and $\mathcal{Z}$ero-to-$\mathcal{T}$en $\mathcal{C}$hart $\mathcal{E}$xercises

Sometimes when we get an answer from our pendulum work, we may want to dig deeper to understand if this answer comes with 100 percent certainty. That is when this percentage chart comes in handy. This chart helps us learn whether something is absolutely, without a doubt, 100 percent right for us at the moment, or perhaps it is not 100 percent optimal. Here's a quick exercise on how to use this chart:

- After sitting down in a quiet space, getting grounded, and calibrating your pendulum, begin your pendulum work by asking a simple question. For example, if you've decided you are going to get your first tattoo (a big and permanent decision for some), you might ask, "Is it in my most optimal interest to get a tattoo?"
- If you get a yes, ask, "Is it 100 percent optimal for me to get a tattoo?" If you get a no, then investigate further with the help of the percentage chart.
- Hold your pendulum at the bottom of the percentage chart in the center. Ask your question and allow the pendulum to begin moving toward a certain percentage number. When you clearly see where the pendulum is swinging, verify by asking the pendulum that the number you are getting is true. If you're getting a 95 percent on your question, then getting a tattoo is still a good idea. Now the fun part—where to put the tattoo!

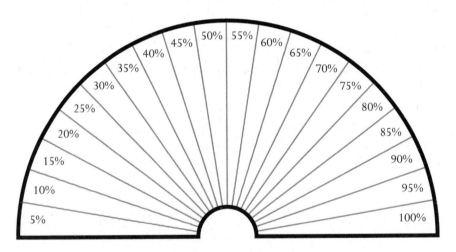

Figure 11: Percentage chart

You can also determine the fit by using a zero-to-ten scale chart. If you are wondering if a certain outfit you chose is a ten out of ten, just use the zero-to-ten scale chart the same way you would use the percentage chart.

This exercise may take practice to get the hang of, but with time, you'll become an expert!

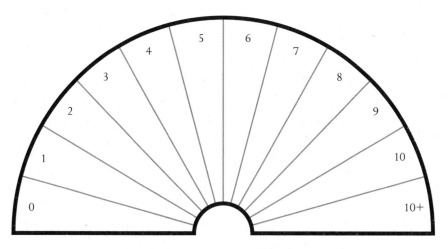

Figure 12: Zero-to-ten scale chart

Alphabet Chart

Use the alphabet chart when you're seeking answers that can be spelled out. For example, if you want to know the names of your spirit guides, this chart can be helpful. Take a moment to find a quiet place and calm your mind. After getting grounded and calibrating your pendulum, hold it over the zero-to-ten chart and ask, "How many letters are in my spirit guide's name?" Once you get your answer, hold your pendulum over the alphabet chart and ask your pendulum to show you the first letter of your guide's name. Then ask for the next letter, and the next. Keep going until you have spelled out the name.

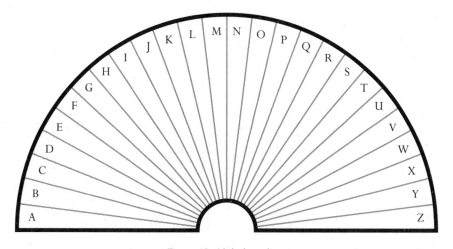

Figure 13: Alphabet chart

Dimensions of Overall Wellness Exercise

There are multiple factors that contribute to how well we feel every day. Our personal values, out current situation, our environment, and the choices we make all influence our sense of well-being at any point in time. This exercise helps us tap into seven dimensions of wellness: physical health, emotional well-being, social wellness and relationships, spiritual connection and life purpose, professional and career satisfaction, environment, and financial well-being. When we understand what area(s) of our life needs more focus, we put ourselves on a path to healing. This awareness is key. These seven dimensions of wellness can help us figure out which batteries might be running low so we can intentionally recharge them. These dimensions of wellness are interconnected. They influence and impact each other to create a more complete sense of overall well-being.

Take a moment to find a quiet place and calm your mind. After calibrating your pendulum, simply hold it over this chart and ask, "What dimension of wellness will enhance my overall well-being?" Slowly move the pendulum over each triangle. When you get a yes movement over a specific triangle, then you have your answer. The most important next step is to reflect and assess why this particular opportunity showed up. Journal and create a plan of how you believe you can improve your wellness in that particular area. Going back to this chart regularly for guidance and acting on the guidance you receive will help you maintain a greater sense of overall wellness.

Figure 14: Dimensions of overall wellness chart

Physical Well-Being Exercise

Focusing on physical well-being can help you maintain a healthy weight and reduce your risk of a number of diseases. Getting adequate sleep, avoiding alcohol, and eating healthy foods can contribute significantly to your well-being. When we are feeling less than optimal on a physical level, this exercise can help you pinpoint what activity to select to get you feeling better.

Take a moment to find a quiet place and calm your mind. After getting grounded and calibrating your pendulum, hold it over this chart and ask, "What is the optimal activity that I can do to shift my physical well-being?" Slowly move the pendulum over each triangle. When you get a yes movement over a specific triangle, then you have your answer.

The most important next step is to perform the activity you've just been guided toward. After you are finished with the activity, pause and notice how your physical well-being has shifted. Are you feeling more energized? Are you more comfortable in your body? This reflection is critical because this is how we learn to create healthy habits that positively shift our physical health. Reflection is your guide toward sticking to healthy habits.

Figure 15: Physical well-being chart

Raise Your Vibration Exercise

We all occasionally experience feeling less than optimal. This feeling may come from mental or physical exhaustion, a difficult interaction with a loved one, or tough news that we need to process. When we experience these difficult feelings, times, or emotions, it is important to shift our perspective and raise our vibration. How can we get ourselves out of the "funk" and move forward so we can show up for ourselves and others with love and positivity?

Resorting to unhealthy behaviors such as stress eating, alcohol consumption, or avoidance typically doesn't yield positive results. What we *can* do is choose a behavior or an action that can help us shift to a better feeling by raising our vibration to a place where we can acknowledge and process the situation objectively. Our subconscious already knows the path to this shift. This simple pendulum exercise will help you narrow in on what step you should take to begin the healing process.

Take a moment to find a quiet place and calm your mind. After getting grounded and calibrating your pendulum, hold it over this chart and ask, "What is the optimal activity that I can do to shift my perspective toward positivity and healing?" Slowly move the pendulum over each triangle. When you get a yes movement over a specific triangle, then you have your answer.

If you get more than one answer, try asking which is the *most* optimal to help you shift your perspective. The most important next step is to perform the activity you've just been guided toward. After you are finished with the activity, pause and notice how your feelings have shifted. Are you experiencing more clarity about the situation? Are you beginning to see the lesson in the experience? This reflection is critical because this is how we learn to create healthy habits that positively shift our outlook. There's magic everywhere. Reflection will surely guide you to see it clearly.

Figure 16: Raise your vibration chart

Embracing Body Positivity Chart

Embracing body positivity is another way to nurture and honor yourself. Body positivity encompasses all aspects of your body and shifts focus to health and wellness rather than outward appearance. Instead of being concerned whether or not our bodies meet societal expectations, body positivity encourages us to honor our bodies by focusing on what they can do.

Focusing on body positivity leads us toward mental, emotional, and physical well-being. If you're looking to honor your body and are not sure how, try using the body positive rituals chart and allow your pendulum to guide you to the most optimal ritual for this moment to embrace your beautiful body and all that it does for you.

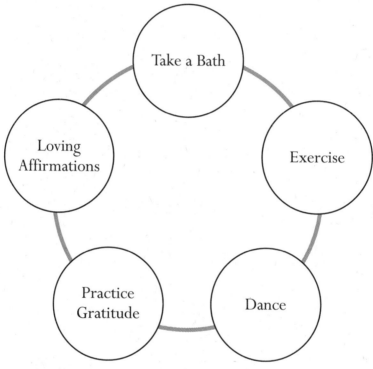

Figure 17: Body positivity chart

What Crystal Should I Work With?

If you're curious about what crystal is most optimal for you to work with on any given day, here's a chart that you can use with your pendulum to figure it out.

1. Collect your crystals and arrange them on the crystal placement grid.
2. After finding a quiet place, getting centered, and calibrating your pendulum, ask, "What crystal is optimal for me to work with today?"

3. Hold your pendulum over each crystal until you get a clear yes movement.

4. If you get more than one yes response, narrow down those that you want to work with and ask the following question of each one. For example, if you've narrowed them down to three, you can ask, "Is lapis lazuli the most optimal crystal for me to work with today versus citrine or aventurine?" You can also ask if working with two of the three crystals, or all of them, is in your best interest at this time. There's no limit.

Figure 18: Crystal placement grid

Make Your Own Chart

Use the following blank templates to create your own charts based on the questions you are exploring with your pendulum.

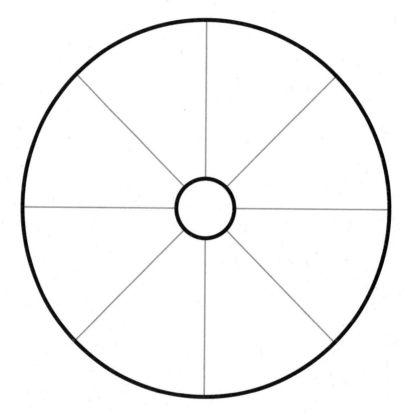

Figure 19: Blank chart

Pendulum Session Guidesheet

The worksheet provided is intended for you to use as a guide when planning a pendulum session. Research shows that when we write down what we're working on, be it our intentions or whatever else, we are better able to retain the information and manifest our desires.[53]

---

53 Mark Murphy, "Neuroscience Explains Why You Need to Write Down Your Goals If You Actually Want to Achieve Them," *Forbes*, April 15, 2018, https://www.forbes.com/sites/markmurphy/2018/04/15/neuroscience-explains-why-you-need-to-write-down-your-goals-if-you-actually-want-to-achieve-them/?sh=66746abc7905.

Make your pendulum practice your own and adjust the worksheet as you'd like. You may not need it all and prefer to use your mind and imagination, and that's great too. Use it as a resource when you need it, especially in conjunction with your journal.

Get Grounded
- How will I get present? What do I need to set aside?
- Who am I inviting to be the source of my answers?
- What is my intention?
- Key questions I'm planning to ask:
  - Is it optimal for me to ...
  - Is it in my highest good and the highest good of all to ...
  -
  -
  -

Calibrate Your Pendulum and Conduct Your Session

Session Reflection
Key Learnings
-
-
-

Action Steps
-
-
-

Give Gratitude for the Guidance

RECOMMENDED RESOURCES

Lana and Karina offer a collection of tools, events, and products for accessing your intuition, personal and professional transformation, self-empowerment, and finding your purpose.

Intuitive Tools and Spiritual Jewelry:
www.hcdivinecreations.com
Individual and Organizational Coaching:
www.heartcentriccoaching.com
Inquiries about presentations and speaking engagements:
info@heartcentriccoaching.com
Instagram, Facebook, and TikTok: @hcdivinecreations

We also recommend the following resources that we found inspirational in our journey:

The Edge Magazine

Features mind, body, and spirit articles, events, and interviews and a partner directory of holistic-living practitioners and services.

https://www.edgemagazine.net

Everett and Charlie Art Gallery

Suzie Marty, owner and curator. Features a wraparound, floor-to-ceiling sampling of original art from more than sixty local Minnesotan artists.

https://www.everettandcharlie.com/

Dana Childs

Dana Childs is a gifted healer and an intuitive. Dana brings forward individual truths that lead to healing and a state of well-being.

https://danachildsintuitive.com/

Om Center of Healing

The OM Center of Healing houses two Harmonic Eggs, which are patented healing chambers. A Harmonic Egg uses sound, light, and vibration to promote healing and wellness.

https://omoftheegg.com/

New World Women

New World Women is a sisterhood of curious women on a spiritual journey. This group promotes self-care and helps women receive financial rewards for incorporating self-care into their lives.

https://www.newworldwomen.com/

Book Recommendations

Bernstein, Gabrielle. *The Universe Has Your Back*. Carlsbad, CA: Hay House, 2018.

Fairchild, Alana. *Messages in the Numbers: The Universe Is Talking to You*. Glen Waverly, Victoria, Australia: Blue Angel, 2015.

Gawain, Shakti. *Living in the Light: Follow Your Inner Guidance to Create a New Life and a New World*. Novato, CA: New World Library, 2011.

Gray, Kyle. *Angel Numbers: The Message and Meaning Behind 11:11 and Other Number Sequences.* Carlsbad, CA: Hay House, 2019.

Jackson, Laura Lynne. *Signs: The Secret Language of the Universe.* New York: Dial Press, 2020.

Kaehr, Shelley. *The Goddess Discovered: Exploring the Divine Feminine Around the World.* Woodbury, MN: Llewellyn Publications, 2023.

———. *Heal Your Ancestors to Heal Your Life: The Transformative Power of Genealogical Regression.* Woodbury, MN: Llewellyn Publications, 2021.

———. *Past Lives in Ancient Lands and Other Worlds: Understand Your Soul's Journey Through Time.* Woodbury, MN: Llewellyn Publications, 2022.

Lagan, Heather Alicia. *Chaldean Numerology for Beginners.* Woodbury, MN: Llewellyn Publications, 2011.

Morningstar, Dawn. *Venerable Women: Transform Ourselves, Transform the World.* Venerable Women, 2016.

Myss, Caroline. *Anatomy of the Spirit: The Seven Stages of Power and Healing.* London: Harmony, 1996.

———. *Through Time Into Healing: Discovering the Power of Regression Therapy to Erase Trauma and Transform Mind, Body, and Relationships.* New York: Fireside, 1993.

Newton, Michael. *Journey of Souls: Case Studies of Life Between Lives.* St. Paul, MN: Llewellyn Publications, 1994.

Schwartz, Robert. *Your Soul's Plan: Discovering the Real Meaning of the Life You Planned Before You Were Born.* Berkeley, CA: North Atlantic Books, 2009.

Singer, Michael A. *The Untethered Soul: The Journey Beyond Yourself.* Oakland, CA: New Harbinger Publications, 2007.

Webster, Richard. *How to Use a Pendulum: 50 Practical Rituals and Spiritual Activities for Clarity and Guidance.* Woodbury, MN: Llewellyn Publications, 2020.

———. *Llewellyn's Complete Book of Divination.* Woodbury, MN: Llewellyn Publications, 2017.

Weiss, Brian. *Many Lives, Many Masters: The True Story of a Prominent Psychiatrist, His Young Patient, and the Past-Life Therapy That Changed Both Their Lives.* New York: Touchstone, 1988.

BIBLIOGRAPHY

Bachler, Käthe. *Earth Radiation.* John Living, 2007.

Beckler, Melanie. "Angelic Hierarchy—Understanding the 9 Angel Ranks." Ask Angels. Accessed September 25, 2023. https://www.ask-angels.com/spiritual-guidance/angelic -hierarchy/.

Bernstein, Gabby. "How to Ask the Universe for a Sign." GabbyBernstein.com. Accessed September 25, 2023. https:// gabbybernstein.com/secret-asking-universe-sign-trusting -guidance-receive/.

Brown, William. "Science: The Physics of a Dowsing Pendulum." *NewScientist*, October 6, 1990. https://www .newscientist.com/article/mg12817373-200-science-the -physics-of-a-dowsing-pendulum/.

Bundson, Andrew, Kenneth Richman, and Elizabeth Kensinger. "Consciousness as a Memory System." *Cognitive and Behavioral Neurology* 25, no. 4 (December 2022): 263–97. doi:10.1097 /WNN.000000000000031.

Calaprice, Alice, ed. *The Ultimate Quotable Einstein.* Princeton, NJ: Princeton University Press, 2011.

"Chakra Basics." International Association of Reiki Professionals. Accessed November 6, 2023. https://iarp.org/chakra-basics/.

"Crystal & Gemstone Therapy." Oriental Healing Oasis and Wellness Center. Accessed September 22, 2023. https://orientalhealingoasis.com /gemstone-crystal-therapy.

Decoz, Hans. "The History and Meaning of Angel Numbers." World Numerology. Accessed September 25, 2023.zzz https://www.worldnumerology .com/blog/angel-numbers.html.

Embogama. "Difference between Conscious and Unconscious Mind." Pediaa. August 5, 2016. https://pediaa.com/difference-between-conscious-and -subconscious-mind/.

Encyclopaedia Britannica. S.v. "Michel-Eugène Chevruel." By Albert B. Costa. Last modified August 27, 2023. https://www.britannica.com/biography /Michel-Eugene-Chevreul.

"The Energetic Heart Is Unfolding." HeartMath. July 22, 2010. https://www .heartmath.org/articles-of-the-heart/science-of-the-heart/the-energetic -heart-is-unfolding/.

"Foucault Pendulum." Smithsonian. Accessed September 21, 2023. https:// www.si.edu/spotlight/foucault-pendulum.

Gaal, Rachel. "June 16, 1657: Christiaan Huygens Patents the First Pendulum Clock." *APS News* 26, no. 6 (June 2017). https://www.aps.org/publications /apsnews/201706/history.cfm.

Gray, Kyle. *Angel Numbers: The Message and Meaning Behind 11:11 and Other Number Sequences.* Carlsbad, CA: Hay House, 2019.

———. *Angel Prayers: Harnessing the Help of Heaven to Create Miracles.* London: Hay House UK, 2018.

———. *Raise Your Vibration: 111 Practices to Increase Your Spiritual Connection.* Carlsbad, CA: Hay House, 2016.

Jobs, Steve. Commencement address. Stanford University. June 12, 2005. https://news.stanford.edu/2005/06/12/youve-got-find-love-jobs-says/.

Johnstone, Michael. *The Book of Divination.* London: Sirius, 2022.

Jung, C. G. *The Collected Works of C. G. Jung: Complete Digital Edition.* Vols. 1–19. Edited by Gerhard Adler and R. F. C. Hull. Princeton, NJ: Princeton University Press, 2014.

London, John. "Facts about Pendulums." Sciencing. Last modified April 24, 2017. https://sciencing.com/pendulums-8538891.html.

Magner, Erin. "Brainwaves—For Better Health, Sleep, and Focus." Well and Good. April 24, 2018. https://www.wellandgood.com/brainwaves-biohack-sleep-health-focus/.

"Master Numbers Hold the Powerful Potential in Numerology." Numerology.com. Accessed September 25, 2023. https://www.numerology.com/articles/your-numerology-chart/core-numbers-numerology/.

Mcleod, Saul. "Freud's Theory of the Unconscious Mind." Simply Psychology. Last modified October 24, 2023. https://www.simplypsychology.org/unconscious-mind.html.

Mechlinski, Joe. "Understanding the Three 'Brains' in Our Body (and Their Critical Role at Work)." Medium. September 5, 2018. https://medium.com/@joemechlinski_9502/understanding-the-three-brains-in-our-body-and-their-critical-role-at-work-d1715ae62bff.

"Meditation and Mindfulness: What You Need to Know." National Center for Complementary and Integrative Health. National Institutes of Health. Last modified June 2022. https://www.nccih.nih.gov/health/meditation-and-mindfulness-what-you-need-to-know.

"Merkaba Symbol." Ancient-Symbols.com. Accessed November 6, 2023. https://www.ancient-symbols.com/symbols-directory/merkaba.html.

Mermet, Abbé. The Principles and Practice of Radiesthesia. Translated by Mark Clement. London: Vincent Stuart, 1959.

Moulik, Sanghamitra. "The Auric Energy Field—What It Means and How You Can See It." Medium. February 23, 2022. https://medium.com/know-thyself-heal-thyself/the-auric-energy-field-what-it-means-and-how-can-you-see-it-d4bd6657baf4.

Murphy, Mark. "Neuroscience Explains Why You Need to Write Down Your Goals If You Actually Want to Achieve Them." Forbes, April 15, 2018. https://www.forbes.com/sites/markmurphy/2018/04/15/neuroscience-explains-why-you-need-to-write-down-your-goals-if-you-actually-want-to-achieve-them/?sh=66746abc7905.

Nail, Thomas. "Most Brain Activity Is Background Noise'—and That's Upending Our Understanding of Consciousness." Salon, February 20, 2021.

https://www.salon.com/2021/02/20/most-brain-activity-is
-background-noise-cognitive-flux-consciousness-brain-activity-research/.

"Numerology Plays a Key Role in Who You're Most Compatible With."
Numerology.com. Accessed September 25, 2023. https://www
.numerology.com/articles/about-numerology/angel-number-meanings/.

Olson, Jay A., Ewalina Jeyanesan, and Amir Raz. "Ask the Pendulum: Personality Predictors of Ideomotor Performance." *Neuroscience of Consciousness* 1
(2017): nix014. https://www.ncbi.nlm.nih.gov/pmc/articles/PMC5858027/.

Percy, Maggie, and Nigel Percy. *Pendulums: For Guidance and Healing.* London:
Flame Tree Publishing, 2021.

Pride Institute. "Pride Institute Awarded Newsweek's Best Addiction Treatment Center Honor for a Second Year Running." September 18, 2021.
https://pride-institute.com/wp-content/uploads/2023/02/Pride-Institute
-Newsweek-Press-Release-2021-1.pdf.

Raven, Hazel. *The Angel Bible.* New York: Sterling Publishing, 2006.

"The Science of HeartMath." HeartMath. Accessed September 19, 2023.
https://www.heartmath.com/science/.

"Science of the Heart: Heart-Brain Communication." HeartMath. Accessed
September 26, 2023. https://www.heartmath.org/research/science-of
-the-heart/heart-brain-communication/.

Slatter, Jean. *Hiring the Heavens: A Practical Guide to Developing Working Relationships with the Spirits of Creation.* Novato, CA: New World Library, 2005.

Talisa and Sam. "Rune Meanings and How to Use Rune Stones for Divination."
Two Wander (blog). Accessed September 25, 2023. https://www.twowander
.com/blog/rune-meanings-how-to-use-runestones-for-divination.

Umoh, Ruth. "Steve Jobs and Albert Einstein Both Attributed Their Extraordinary Success to This Personality Trait." CNBC. Last modified June 30, 2017.
https://www.cnbc.com/2017/06/29/steve-jobs-and-albert-einstein-both
-attributed-their-extraordinary-success-to-this-personality-trait.html.

Van Helden, Al. "Pendulum Clock." The Galileo Project. Accessed September
21, 2023. http://galileo.rice.edu/sci/instruments/pendulum.html.

Walters, Meg. "Healing Crystals: What They Can and Can't Do." Healthline. July 20, 2023. https://www.healthline.com/health/healing-crystals-what-they-can-do-and-what-they-cant.

Webster, Richard. *Pendulum Magic for Beginners*. St. Paul, MN: Llewellyn Publications, 2002.

Winfrey, Oprah. "What Oprah Knows for Sure about Trusting Her Intuition." *O, The Oprah Magazine*, August 2011. https://www.oprah.com/spirit/oprah-on-trusting-her-intuition-oprahs-advice-on-trusting-your-gut.

Woods, Walt. *Letter to Robin*. 10th ed. Oroville, CA: The Print Shoppe, 2001. https://lettertorobin.files.wordpress.com/2016/06/rbn_10_4_english.pdf.

Youngblood, Lloyd. "Dowsing: An Ancient History." American Society of Dowsers. Accessed September 21, 2023. https://dowsers.org/dowsing-history/.

"Zhang Heng." New World Encyclopedia. Accessed September 21, 2023. https://www.newworldencyclopedia.org/entry/Zhang_Heng.

About the Authors

Karina Muller

My story begins in Communist Russia, behind the iron curtain. I was born in St. Petersburg (Leningrad at the time of my birth) under the Communist regime. As a young child, I was always drawn to nature and treasured the time that I spent running around in the woods during my summers in Lithuania.

When I was ten years old, my parents, my grandparents, and I immigrated to the United States. We were blessed to have the opportunity to leave Russia and start new lives. I learned to speak English and worked very hard to fit in as a young middle schooler. I was still unique and different from my peers. I thought that becoming just like everyone else would be my key to happiness. It took me until my adulthood to come to the realization that standing out from the crowd is a blessing. I learned to honor and cherish my uniqueness.

During my college and graduate school years, I pursued gaining as much business knowledge as possible. Getting the top jobs and promotions was exciting for a little while but did not give me any deep satisfaction and peace in my heart-center. I spent many years working for companies in leadership roles and eventually moved into becoming an independent consultant, helping business leaders solve complex issues. I loved being a trusted advisor and providing guidance on how to solve their most challenging business problems. Essentially, I was acting as their business consultant and life coach. The coaching part of my work gave me so much joy and satisfaction. I watched my clients prosper as they became empowered and self-assured. Guiding my clients to tap into their intuition was always a key component of my coaching work.

After three decades in corporate America, I pursued a life coaching certification. I met Lana through our coaching certification program with Learning Journeys, the International Center of Coaching. Lana and I realized that we were very aligned in our values of empowering our clients to live their truths and pursue the most optimal path forward.

My professional life started merging with my interests and passions in forming HeartCentric Coaching Collaborative and HeartCentric Divine Creations with Lana. Instead of work being work, my career transformed into joyful daily pursuits. I noticed that every task I pursued was filled with excitement, joy, and fun. These positive feelings reinforced that I was living out my purpose and listening to my intuition. The universe is always conspiring to let me know that the work I'm doing is needed, meaningful, and making a difference. For the first time in my life, I am experiencing what it is like to live each day walking on my most optimal path.

I hold an MBA from the University of Minnesota and a BS from Indiana University in business. My certification as a life coach practitioner is from Learning Journeys (ICF accredited).

Lana Gendlin

Similar to Karina's story, mine begins in the same part of the world. I was born in the former Soviet Union, in Minsk, the capital of what is now Belarus. My parents decided they wanted freedom for themselves and their two young daughters, and we left for the United States when I was two and a half years old. While I have no recollection of Russia, other than from my visit to Moscow in 2008, I do know that I am very grateful for the sacrifices my parents made to start a new life. From the stories they have shared, I know that their journey was quite difficult. However, what I took away from their struggles are examples of courage, perseverance, strength, resilience, and how to push through fear and go for your dreams.

As a young child, I remember being wildly imaginative and creative. I loved playing "store" and also pretending I was a journalist writing books and advertising campaigns. I would write stories and scripts, draw them out on storyboards, and then line them up near the edge of my bed and act them out. I also used to record myself on my pink boombox using cassette tapes and pretended to have my own radio show. This was beyond fun for me!

Throughout my childhood, I grew increasingly curious about the world around me, what makes people different from one another, what makes us alike, our cultures, our languages, our foods, our ceremonies—basically, what makes us human. I remember watching shows and reading various books and *National Geographic* magazines about human origins, Neanderthals, ancient civilizations, and anything having to do with anthropology. It was fascinating to me, and I couldn't get enough.

My love for other cultures and life's great mysteries, coupled with an inner knowing that there is much to understand beyond what we can see, led me to pursue degrees in anthropology, journalism, and museum studies. Throughout my studies in college and graduate school, I had the chance to deepen my love for helping people connect and thereby understand themselves.

Oftentimes, when my coaching clients are lost or stuck about what their purpose in life is, I ask them what they loved to do as a child. Typically, this is where we find our true nature—the uninhibited state of being before we begin absorbing others' ideas of what's right for us. I know that oftentimes we lose our way on the course to adulthood. I've seen this firsthand in my career working in arts and culture institutions and through my own life experiences. This is true for the artist in all of us, and for many others, whose dreams don't always come to fruition because society has taught us to live by values that are not our own. But if we go back to what we loved as young children, when being uninhibited and doing what felt joyful to us was second nature, we find our true purpose.

My path to finding my purpose did not happen quickly and easily. We all have a story. We all endure hardships and happy periods in life. I have found that my struggles have happened *for* me and not *to* me. Every moment, twist, and "diversion" has led me to this point. I experienced extreme loss in a short timeframe in my mid-thirties—the loss of a child to stillbirth, the loss of a career in museums that had been my livelihood, and the loss of my marriage via divorce—all within three months. The deep grief and vulnerability I was feeling at that time kept moving me toward exploring my inner world. It was from a place of feeling buried that seeds were being planted. I didn't realize it at the time, but my darkest days were my biggest learning opportunities to move my life forward in a way that was for my highest good. When I think back to how I got through that "dark night of the soul" and where I am today, it's clear that my losses, and what I thought were failures, were the universe's way of redirecting me on my most optimal path.

After finding success working in world-renowned cultural institutions, museums, nonprofits, corporate, startups, and launching several businesses, I was searching for something deeper. I began working with a life coach. It was that transformational experience that inspired me to pursue a life coaching certification myself. What I realized is that, unbeknownst to me, I had been coaching colleagues, clients, and interns informally for many years.

Meeting Karina while obtaining my coaching certification was certainly part of a larger plan. At first, she and I had no idea that we were both from the same part of the world and had such parallel life stories. During a random conversation with a few friends, we accidentally discovered that we both speak Russian and came to this country as immigrants in the same year. We also shared the same passion and drive to help people achieve their version of success and fulfillment. If we are receptive and open, synchronicities show up in our lives constantly!

It seems that life has come full circle. As an entrepreneur, I own an online store and write marketing and educational materials. I also speak on podcasts and in front of live audiences. I am grateful that I get to coach others and help them discover who they are, while continuing to achieve personal growth and exploring my spirituality.

Helping others discover their innate creativity and enabling them to connect with their wisdom fuels my soul to no end. Being a part of people's transformational experiences using a beautiful, handmade pendulum is life-changing for them and me. I absolutely love designing, creating, and sharing the power of the pendulum with the world. It is remarkable knowing that I am doing a small part to help impact the lives of so many in a positive way. Listening to my inner wisdom and connecting to the creative power inside of me continues to be where I find solace. Helping others do the same is my heart's work.

When I'm not playing at work, I enjoy spending time with my family and Siberian Husky, reading, making jewelry, learning about the healing arts, and any form of exercise. I hold an MA from George Washington University in museum studies and anthropology and a BS from the University of Minnesota, Twin Cities, in anthropology and journalism and mass communications. My certification as a life coach practitioner is from Learning Journeys, the International Center of Coaching (ICF accredited).

NOTES

To Write to the Authors

If you wish to contact the authors or would like more information about this book, please write to the authors in care of Llewellyn Worldwide Ltd. and we will forward your request. Both the authors and the publisher appreciate hearing from you and learning of your enjoyment of this book and how it has helped you. Llewellyn Worldwide Ltd. cannot guarantee that every letter written to the author can be answered, but all will be forwarded. Please write to:

Karina Muller and Lana Gendlin
℅ Llewellyn Worldwide
2143 Wooddale Drive
Woodbury, MN 55125-2989
Please enclose a self-addressed stamped envelope for reply,
or $1.00 to cover costs. If outside the U.S.A., enclose
an international postal reply coupon.

You can also email Lana and Karina at info@heartcentriccoaching.com. Many of Llewellyn's authors have websites with additional information and resources. For more information, please visit our website at http://www.llewellyn.com.